Praise for UNAPOLOGETICALLY AMBITIOUS

"In a world that too often tells women, especially Black women, to stay small, keep quiet, and know their limits, this book says otherwise. It's a celebration of women knowing their power."
—Sheryl Sandberg, COO of Facebook and founder of LeanIn.org and OptionB.org

"Shellye's life story, and the lessons it carries, are powerful examples of focus and ambition that can shape your life for the better. If your goal is just to be famous, maybe this is not the story for you, but if your goal is to be a truly great leader of men and women, you have found your guide."
—Ben Horowitz, *New York Times* bestselling author of *The Hard Thing about Hard Things*

"Through a compelling story about her own journey, Shellye offers powerful tips for how to live life courageously and go after what you want. From investing in your financial health to integrating work, marriage, parenthood, and self-care—each chapter lays out actionable strategies to help you achieve your goals. A must-read for anyone looking for ways to grow and live their best life."
—Thasunda Brown Duckett, CEO of Chase Consumer Banking

"UNAPOLOGETICALLY AMBITIOUS is a treasure trove of strategic wisdom and practical tips, brought to life through amazing storytelling that will leave the reader inspired, empowered, and appreciative. The book deals with the realities of setbacks, trade-offs, and societal norms in an authentic way, while illustrating that strength and success often lie in mind-set and the team you choose in life. The closing chapter serves as a master guide to navigating life, providing a penultimate takeaway for any reader early in their journey to put the wisdom and experience of Archambeau's lessons learned into immediate action!"

—Brad D. Smith, executive chairman of Intuit and Nordstrom

"A successful career in any industry is always underpinned by a few important elements: focus, risk awareness, and drive. Shellye's book UNAPOLOGETICALLY AMBITIOUS underscores the importance these elements can play in your career and showcases brilliant strategies and approaches through her own career pursuits."

—John Thompson, chairman of Microsoft

"Shellye Archambeau is one of the most intelligent, hardworking, and focused women I have met in my forty-plus years of business. I was very pleased to have her join the Verizon board in 2013 and have watched her rise within the board to now head the Corporate Governance Committee. Her experience as an African American woman rising through the ranks of both large global businesses and technology startups gives her a unique perspective to share with those entering the business world, especially those people of color. Grab a pen and paper as you read this book. It is full of the guidance that will put you on a path to career success."

—Lowell McAdam, former CEO of Verizon

"There are lots of people who have the raw talent and ambition to be great successes but lack a strategy and plan. That's what UNAPOLOGETICALLY AMBITIOUS is about! It reveals Shellye Archambeau's formula for developing your own talent and getting what you want out of life both professionally and personally. It's the book I wish I had read when I was in my twenties."

—Eric Schmidt, Google CEO and chairman from 2001–11, Google executive chairman from 2011–15, and Alphabet executive chairman from 2015–18

"Shellye Archambeau is an extraordinary leader whose insight is only rivaled by her foresight. She takes us through her fascinating life's journey, which is marked by dogged persistence, bucking of norms, and repeated excellence. This deeply personal and engaging book is a must-read!"

—Tsedal Neeley, Harvard Business School professor and author of the *Language of Global Success*

"Archambeau's book is essential reading for anyone seeking guidance on taking a strategic approach to increasing their odds for success in business and life. I especially recommend it to entrepreneurs and innovators who are early in their careers and focused on drawing down risk and achieving targeted milestones."

—Clare Leinweber, executive director of the Tsai Center for Innovative Thinking at Yale

Unapologetically Ambitious

Take Risks, Break Barriers, and Create Success on Your Own Terms

Shellye Archambeau
Foreword by Ben Horowitz

GRAND CENTRAL
PUBLISHING

NEW YORK   BOSTON

Grand Central Publishing
Hachette Book Group
1290 Avenue of the Americas, New York, NY 10104
grandcentralpublishing.com
twitter.com/grandcentralpub

First Edition: October 2020

Grand Central Publishing is a division of Hachette Book Group, Inc. The Grand Central Publishing name and logo is a trademark of Hachette Book Group, Inc.

The publisher is not responsible for websites (or their content) that are not owned by the publisher.

The Hachette Speakers Bureau provides a wide range of authors for speaking events. To find out more, go to www.hachettespeakersbureau.com or call (866) 376-6591.

Library of Congress Cataloging-in-Publication Data
Names: Archambeau, Shellye, author.
Title: Unapologetically ambitious : take risks, break barriers, and create
    success on your own terms / Shellye Archambeau ; foreword by Ben
    Horowitz.
Description: First edition. | New York : Grand Central Publishing, [2020] |
    Includes bibliographical references. | Summary: "Full of empowering
    wisdom from one of high tech's first female African American CEOs, this
    inspiring leadership book for readers of Dare to Lead and Start with Why
    offers a blueprint for how to achieve your personal and professional
    goals, drawn from the author's own compelling story of how she weathered
    life's difficulties to build massive success"-- Provided by publisher.
Identifiers: LCCN 2020014850 | ISBN 9781538702895 (hardcover) | ISBN
    9781538702901 (ebook)
Subjects: LCSH: Success in business. | Success. | Ambition. |
    Self-realization.
Classification: LCC HF5386 .A684 2020 | DDC 650.1--dc23
LC record available at https://lccn.loc.gov/2020014850

ISBNs: 978-1-5387-0289-5 (hardcover), 978-1-5387-0290-1 (ebook)

Printed in the United States of America

LSC-C

10 9 8 7 6 5 4 3 2 1

Contents

CONTENTS

Foreword

I first came to know Shellye Archambeau when I hired her to run marketing for my company, Loudcloud. The company was growing much faster than the current team and I could handle; I needed someone with better leadership skills than I had to help build out the organization. Shellye turned out to be just that. During her tenure, she taught me how to make hard decisions and communicate them clearly and unapologetically. In many ways, she was my mentor rather than vice versa.

Eventually, the Loudcloud business didn't work, and Shellye and I parted ways. I remember thinking at the time that wherever she went, they would be quite lucky to have her.

A few months later, Shellye told me that she was considering becoming CEO of a company called Zaplet. This surprised me, because of Zaplet's backstory. Led by Silicon Valley superstar Alan Baratz, Zaplet had once been the darling of the technology world. Baratz had raised gigantic amounts of money and garnered glowing press coverage. Everyone expected Zaplet to be the next great technology company. But as so often happens in technology, things did not go as planned. The company rapidly burned through its massive cash hoard and was on the verge of a total wipeout. In order to save itself from bankruptcy, Zaplet laid off huge numbers of employees and battened down the hatches for what looked like would be a long winter followed by a fire sale.

Companies like Zaplet almost never come back, because they become fatally tainted by their meteoric rise and even swifter fall. Every potential employee, customer, and investor would know the company was damaged goods, and it would be nearly impossible for a new CEO to fight through that. I did not want to see Shellye jump into such a polluted swamp.

I said, "Shellye, I don't think you should take that job." I could tell from her body language that she heard me but wasn't planning to listen to me.

Her reaction was so sharp I worried she thought I was telling her that she *couldn't* do it, when I was really trying to say that she *shouldn't* do it. But as the discussion went on, I realized that Shellye understood the issues and, to a large extent, those issues were the very reason she wanted to be the CEO.

Shellye wasn't optimizing for a personal financial outcome, glory, or a career boost. She was looking for the ultimate test of her leadership skills. She was like a great boxer who wanted to fight the most dangerous opponents to prove she was the best. She was attracted to, rather than repelled by, the insanely high degree of difficulty that Zaplet posed.

Shellye took the job, and Zaplet was as advertised. For every issue that I warned her about, there were another hundred that I did not anticipate. But like Muhammad Ali taking on Joe Frazier and George Foreman, Shellye scratched, clawed, and willed her way to victory. She changed everything about the company: the technology, the business they were in, and most of the employees. She merged it into MetricStream and grew the combined entity into a robust industry leader over fourteen long years.

As I watched her do it, I often wondered where that incredible determination, focus, and will to win came from. Finally, with this book, I have the answer.

Shellye's life story, and the lessons it carries, are powerful examples of focus and ambition that can shape your life for the better. If your goal is just to be famous, maybe this is not the story for you, but if your goal is to be a truly great leader of men and women, you have found your guide.

Ben Horowitz
Co-Founder and General Partner, Andreessen Horowitz

Introduction

I'm in my office at MetricStream Inc., hurriedly clearing a backlog of voice mails, trying to get through them before my first meeting of the day. As usual, they're all sales pitches—cold calls from vendors who don't know who else to approach in the company, so they leave a message for the CEO. Anyone who really needs me calls my cell phone or sends me an email, so I'm only half attending, listening to each message just long enough to confirm that it's a sales call before I delete it. My gaze wanders out the window of my corner office, to the view of Highway 101 in the distance, all those cars rushing who knows where. Outside my door, I hear people arriving at their desks, settling in for another busy day. *What time is it?* I wonder, but before I can check the clock, a distinctive voice interrupts my thoughts: "Shellye, this is Lowell McAdam," the message says.

Lowell McAdam, I think. *Where have I heard that name?*

"Marc Andreessen suggested I talk to you. Can you give me a call?"

Marc Andreessen? Now, that name I know well. What's this about?

I hang up the phone and turn to my computer. A Google

search tells me Lowell McAdam is the relatively new CEO of Verizon, a Fortune 15 company.

Okay…He wouldn't be calling me for MetricStream business purposes, because Verizon isn't a client or a prospect. What could this be about? Why would Marc refer Lowell to me? Is this a job opportunity? Does he want me to do a speaking engagement?

Befuddled, I call Marc.

"It's all good, Shellye," Marc tells me. "Lowell's looking for a new board member with experience that matches yours, a high-profile CEO in tech who has managed operations at scale. I recommended he speak with you."

I hang up the phone. Verizon wants to talk to me about a board position? A smile takes over my face.

When I was a junior in high school, after a fateful conversation with a school guidance counselor, I set a major career goal: I wanted to become a CEO. During college, I refined that goal: I would become CEO of a tech company. On my way toward earning my CEO seat, I learned there was a governance structure one step above the CEO: the board of directors—the people who hire and fire CEOs and who ensure a company's shareholders see returns on their investments. So I added another goal: I wanted to serve on a Fortune 500 board before I was fifty-five.

Now, at fifty years old, after ten years as CEO of MetricStream, I'm getting the call from Verizon. A momentary doubt enters my mind: *But am I ready for a Fortune 50 board position?* I recognize that voice, and I know better than to listen to it. *Am I ready? Of course I am. I've been working my whole life for this. All the strategic planning, discipline, and hard trade-offs are paying off.*

After a brief conversation with Lowell, I know I want the board seat. The minute I get off the phone, as I've always done in moments like this, I call my husband, Scotty, to share the exciting news.

"Babe, guess what?" I say when he answers.

"What?" he asks, his voice bright with anticipation.

"I just talked to Lowell McAdam from Verizon." I can't shake the smile off my face when I say it: "They're interested in me as a potential board member. So, it'll be a process, but I'm going for it. We'll see what happens . . ."

Then Scotty, my number one cheerleader, says, "What do you mean we'll see? You know he's going to want you on the board after he meets you."

Scotty was right.

⌐

As an African American woman in my fifties, I don't exactly fit the prototype for a tech industry business leader. I can't tell you how many times people—especially women and people of color—have asked me this question: How did you get where you are?

You may be wondering the same thing.

Before I answer the question, let me tell you a bit about where I started. In 1962, I was born into a family of modest means and high ambitions. This was not long after lunch counter sit-ins called national attention to segregation, and not long before Martin Luther King Jr. delivered his "I Have a Dream" speech at the March on Washington.

During the first five years of my life, the Civil Rights Act passed, peaceful demonstrators met brutality on the Edmund Pettus Bridge in Selma, Alabama, the Voting Rights Act banned practices that limited voter rights, and racial tensions soared. In this environment, my determined parents set out to make a life for our family, following opportunity wherever it took us.

As for me, I started as a shy, gangly black girl in an all-white elementary school, and I grew into a successful high school student and a graduate of the Wharton School. I met a wonderful man to share my life with, and together we raised a family. After a fast-paced rise through the ranks at IBM, I became one of very (*very*) few female African American CEOs in the technology sector, all the way back in 2003, when I was forty years old. As CEO of Zaplet, I orchestrated a merger with MetricStream, guided our combined company through the choppy waters of the dot-com bust and the financial crisis of 2008, and MetricStream came out the other end an industry leader, employing over a thousand people. Along the way, I have mentored countless young professionals, and I have been involved in organizations that do a lot of good—especially for minorities and women.

How did I get here? That's what this book is all about—the values, experiences, lessons, ideas, strategies, and actions that got me where I am today. If I had to sum it up, though, I would say ambition got me here—ambition supported by the conscious choices I made every step of the way.

Success begins with figuring out what you want, then making the choices that will get you there. You'll notice I use that word a lot: *choices.*

Early on, my parents set me on the right track by teaching me the foundational life skills and lessons that would help me survive in a world hostile to young black girls like me. I'll share those with you in Part One, "Early Lessons." (Spoiler alert: Some of those early lessons I still put to good use today.)

In my college years, I developed a life plan that would ultimately serve me through the next three decades. You'll read about that in Part 2, "Strategize for Success." I mean, I planned *everything* out: my marriage, kids, career path, even my future lifestyle. I will tell you how I set myself up to accomplish everything on that list (give or take a detail or two), and how you can do that, too.

In Part 3, "Living the Plan," I'll recount the challenges I faced and the wisdom I gained while executing my life plan, stepping into my roles as career woman, wife, and mother. It's not easy, let me tell you, managing all that, but you can do it if you make smart choices in accordance with your plan.

Of course, life never goes *exactly* as planned. But you don't have to tumble out of your boat just because the river bends. In Part 4, "Swerve," I'll talk about how I made necessary changes while holding tight to my goals.

Finally, in Part 5, "Improving Your Odds," I'll share my top five, tried-and-true tips for advancing in your career and achieving your life goals.

Now, in addition to *choices*, you may have noticed I use another word a lot: *plan.*

That's right. I'm a planner. Big-time. In fact, some might say I'm a little over the top when it comes to strategizing my life. But honestly, as a business leader and mentor, I'm surprised how many people—smart, talented, creative people—*don't* have a plan in place to help them reach their goals.

I know people who have taken the opportunities they found right in front of them, instead of strategizing to create their own options. I've watched people make easy choices that don't truly serve their long-term goals. I've met people who once had an idea—a far-fetched dream—of what they wanted, but they never formalized that dream into a goal or figured out a plan to get there. These are the folks who wake up in midlife, wondering how they ended up so far away from where they'd hoped they would be.

All too often, I meet people who don't think about the long term at all. If you don't have goals, how will you reach them? If you have goals but no plan, how will you know if you're on track?

The good news is: It's never too early to plan. And the better news is: It's never too late. At any point in your life or career, you can set an objective, research the skills, experiences, or resources you need to go after it, and then map out a plan to achieve it.

Seriously.

I'm not the only person who has custom-built a happy, successful life. You can do it, too. This doesn't mean you won't face challenges, disappointments, and tragedies along the way. (Most of us do.) It means that you can make life—and everything that comes with it—work for you.

Wait—are you wondering if this actually applies to you? If *you* can find success and happiness? Why is this a question so many of us ask ourselves—not "How can I get what I want?" but "Is this even possible for someone like me?"

Let me say, unequivocally, yes. Yes, it is.

Let me explain.

If you haven't figured this out already, I'm an ambitious woman. Unapologetically so. When people ask me where my ambition comes from, well, it's sort of like asking me where my legs came from. It grew with me; it's part of my genetic code. Just as you can trace certain physical traits back through the generations of my family, so can you trace ambition.

My aunt Dee, keeper of the family papers on my mother's side, has a document that reminds me how far my family has come over the years. Yellowed parchment, faded brown ink—it's called a deed of manumission, a handwritten letter penned by a slave owner, verifying the release of one of my ancestors from slavery. To read it, you would have no idea it referred to a human being. It could be a description of livestock—male, five feet five inches, high forehead, long scar on his neck. Just a couple generations later, my great-grandfather, a proud and accomplished man whom everyone called Papa, was bringing my mother and her sister to lunch counter sit-ins, teaching them to take a stand for what's right, and writing weekly letters to the editor of the local paper, speaking out against injustice.

On my father's side, we have a family Bible, a heavy tome bound in blue cloth embossed with intricate gold lettering. Inside, it's inscribed with the names and birthdates of ancestors, beginning with Dominique D'Archambau (a different spelling of my last name), a sea captain from France, who married a Jamaican woman named Maria Chaddenne who gave birth to Thomas Nicholas, in 1806, in Jamaica. That list of names leads right to my own grandchildren. Tracing my finger down the page, I imagine what life was like for each generation. I see how each name is like a rung on a ladder climbing toward greater and greater freedoms.

Yes, I see the challenges my ancestors faced. I also see their strength—the work ethic, pride, faith, and ambition that propelled them forward. That's in my DNA.

As for you? No matter where you are starting, no matter where you or your family have been, you too have the strength to propel yourself forward. If you're skeptical, that's okay. Stick with me. I'll walk you through it.

So, are you ready? Let's start with some questions:

What do you want from life?

What values do you live by?

What sort of lifestyle do you seek?

What fulfills you?

These are the questions I want you to ask yourself. Now, no two individuals want the same things out of life. We all know this in theory, but when it comes time to design our lives, sometimes we overlook that essential question: What do *I* want? Forget about achieving success as someone else defines it. What do *you* want?

By the end of this book, I hope you will both define what you want and feel empowered to go after it, unapologetically.

PART ONE

EARLY LESSONS

1

Create Your Own Luck

I. Am. CEO.

Snapping my eyes open in the predawn darkness of my bedroom, my husband sleeping quietly beside me, I hear this thought reverberating through my mind as loud as Fourth of July fireworks, ricocheting off every corner of my brain: *I. Am. CEO.* It is way too early to be awake, but I can no longer pretend sleep is an option for me on this Monday, my first day in my new role.

I take a deep breath and exhale, trying to calm myself. Not wanting to let this extraordinary moment slip past, I close my eyes and assess my feelings. A single question filters into my consciousness: *How did I get here?*

I chuckle softly into the quiet. It's a silly question. It's not as if I dropped down into this moment out of the blue. I walked every single painstaking step it took to get here. I spent decades learning, growing, planning, overcoming, strategizing, making intentional choices, taking calculated risks, and working hard—really, *really* hard—to get to this exact place.

But somehow, I am amazed to have arrived.

So amazed that I want to go back to the beginning and watch it all happen again.

How, exactly, did I get here?

⌣

When I was six years old, my family spent Christmas in a hotel room in downtown Los Angeles. Mom, Dad, my two sisters, my baby brother, and me, all bursting with holiday excitement as we ripped open presents and ate Christmas cookies before breakfast. For us kids, that Christmas morning was as wonderful as any other, though I wouldn't find out for years just how much grit had made that holiday happen.

My dad, Lester Archambeau, worked for IBM, a company known for transferring employees all over the country. In my short life, my family had already moved four times—from Washington, DC, to Boston; to Lexington, Kentucky, to Philadelphia—and now we were headed to Granada Hills, a nice suburb of Los Angeles, in the San Fernando Valley. Moving all the time like that could have felt dramatic to another family, but my parents didn't deal in drama; they dealt in reality. They just figured out how to make things work. They also held tight to their core values while making these moves. For example, my parents believed in a good education, so when my dad was transferred to California, my mom, Mera Archambeau, refused to let me miss a single day of first grade. Instead, my father moved ahead of us, I stayed in school through December 23, and on Christmas Eve 1968, we up and flew across the country, on IBM's dime.

I should mention here that Mom had decided to have all her kids as fast as she could. She said she wanted to be done with diapers in one stretch. So I was born in July of 1962, Lindy in May of 1964, Niki in August of 1965, and Arch was born in June of 1967, before my fifth birthday. When I think of my mom, flying cross-country with four children age six and under—how she handled that I will never know, but that's my point: She handled it. That's what my mom does, and by example, that's what she has taught me to do.

Our house wouldn't be ready for us when we arrived in California, which is how we ended up in a hotel. This arrangement had been a matter of serious concern for Lindy and Niki: not moving, not staying in a hotel, but the logistics of *Christmas*.

"Mommy," Lindy had whined, a few days before our move, "Santa can't find us if we move! We won't get any presents this year!"

Before Mom could answer, I chimed in. Because at six years old, I clearly knew everything already. "Don't worry!" I assured Lindy. "Santa Claus knows everything, remember? That's how he knows if we are good or not. He sees the people who are flying, too. He will know we're in California, and he'll bring Christmas to us there. You'll see!"

My proclamation may have put my sisters at ease, but meanwhile, my mother was panicking. Christmas is Mom's favorite holiday. She and Dad had a tradition of doing everything—baking cookies, putting up the tree, wrapping presents—late on Christmas Eve, after we had gone to bed. Just imagine this:

Each year, we would go to bed on Christmas Eve in a normal house. It could have been July, given the lack of any sign of the winter holiday. On Christmas morning, we would wake up to find stockings hanging from our bedroom doorknobs, filled with little toys and candy canes. That's how we knew Santa had come. After going through our stockings, we would rush downstairs to witness magic.

Before we could see it, we would hear it. Mom had the Christmas music playing. The staircase was wrapped in garland with sparkling ornaments hanging at each loop. We saw the reflection of blinking lights before the tree came into view. The dining room table featured a huge centerpiece made up of pinecones, evergreen branches, and fruit. As we entered the living room, it seemed alive with Christmas spirit—every surface laden with decorations. Personalized, homemade, decorative knitted stockings for each of us hung from the mantel, on top of which perched a sled filled with presents and pulled by reindeer. A winter wonderland scene, complete with fake snow. Tiered trays of Christmas cookies sat on the end tables, surrounded by decorative snowmen, Santa Clauses, and elves. The lampshades were draped in Christmas fabric, and the curtains were accented with silver garland and twinkling lights. Finally, the tree: as tall as the ceiling, loaded with ornaments from homemade to porcelain, circled by piles of presents. Mom and Dad had told us Santa was responsible for delivering this miracle, and we eagerly believed. Santa could do anything; we had proof.

The year we moved to California, Mom had been planning to downsize the production—until my confident assessment of Santa's abilities set the expectations for everyone: full production, on location, in California. Not only was Mom now on the hook for presents, she also had to turn a two-bedroom hotel room into a Christmas wonderland—after a cross-country flight, in a strange town, overnight, while her children slept.

At this point, you might be thinking Mom would choose to compromise, or even to end the fairy tale. But you don't know my mother. No, instead she created a plan and enlisted help to execute it. She shared her dilemma with the moving van driver, who stepped up to help her. Our gifts and the boxes of decorations would be loaded on the truck last, so they could come off first. He would bring the truck to the hotel late on Christmas Eve to drop off the goods, plus some homemade cookies his wife would bake. Meanwhile, our family members helped mail the rest of the gifts to the hotel, so they'd be waiting at the desk when we arrived. Just like that, Mom had everything taken care of, except the tree.

On Christmas Eve, after a flight that must have felt a lot longer to Mom than it did to my siblings and me, we met Dad at the airport. He loaded us up in a rented station wagon and drove us to the hotel. After a hurried dinner, we kids dutifully went to bed, imagining Santa Claus and his reindeer on their way.

Meanwhile, the real Santa went to work retrieving presents and decorations, while Dad drove through downtown Los Angeles in search of a Christmas tree. With no cell phone, no Google Maps, no Amazon or TaskRabbit to help, he drove for a long time, scanning the streets for anything that might work. As far as he could tell, every last store was closed for the holiday. It was getting late, and Dad was getting desperate, when he spotted a hardware store with its lights on. In the window: a fully decorated Christmas tree, and a sign that said CLOSED.

Dad knew this was his one chance. He parked, walked up

7

to the door, and started pounding on it. A man came out of the back and waved at him: *Go away.* But nobody tells Lester Archambeau where to go, especially when he's trying to get something done for his family. He kept pounding.

Finally, the man came to the door and opened it a crack. "Can't you read?" he said. "Sign says we're closed."

My dad quickly wedged his foot in the door. "Mister, I want to buy your Christmas tree in the window there."

"It's not for sale," the man said, and tried to close the door. Of course, Dad's foot was blocking it.

"Please," Dad said. "I've got four little kids in a hotel room, and they're expecting Santa Claus to bring them a tree. Can't you let me buy it from you? I'll even bring it right back after Christmas."

I don't know of many real-life Christmas miracles, but for my dad, this was one. The man relented, and somehow Dad returned to the hotel with a fully decorated tree.

The next morning, we woke to find stockings on our door-knob. Santa had found us! I threw open the bedroom door and there they were: the blinking lights on the Christmas tree, Santas and elves on the end tables, garland around the windows, trays of cookies, and gifts around the tree.

"See?" I said to my sisters and brother. "I told you Santa would know where we were."

My poor parents. Once I grew older and learned the truth about Santa, Mom and Dad allowed me to sneak downstairs and help create the overnight Christmas magic. For the first time, I understood the near-impossible situation I'd put them in at the hotel. Mom and Dad always loved me just as I was— a take-charge, ambitious, no-nonsense girl—but they never did let me live that one down.

As you can see, Mom and Dad were a determined pair, and they were particularly determined to raise each of their children with a good life, a strong character, and a great education. Reaching these goals required both creative planning and the discipline to stick with the plan.

Dad was the money earner in our family. Every day, he dressed in a suit, white shirt, and tie, and commuted an hour each way to his job at IBM. He didn't have a college degree, but he was smart and a natural engineer. He could build or fix anything. Years earlier, he had landed a job repairing typewriters for IBM, and he ultimately worked his way up to branch manager in the service division.

Mom, who did have a college education, and skills ranging from crafting to finance, chose to be a stay-at-home mom. It was their expectation and that of the times. Like my father, she too was ambitious. Now, most people tie ambition to career attainment, but I see ambition differently. To me, ambition means working hard, with determination, to get what you want from life. Mom had that in spades.

Together, my parents' goal was to raise well-educated, well-adjusted kids who could support themselves and do whatever they wanted in life. As my father has said many times, Mom was the drill sergeant of the family, maintaining order and discipline. She kept everybody on task and on budget and having fun besides. She was endlessly resourceful in making our family tick. She delegated household responsibilities to each of us kids. On Dad's payday, she doled out allowances to everyone, including my father. Maintaining a strict budget, she found a way to fund activities, from sports to Girl Scouts to horseback riding, all while saving toward college for us kids. On a single salary, that wasn't easy, but my parents managed it.

And we did have fun. We loved to play games: Candy Land, Sorry!, Yahtzee, Go Fish, War, and Spit. We loved make-believe and running around outside. But most of all we loved wrestling matches with Dad after he came home from work. He'd try and get all four of us pinned to the floor simultaneously. Most days, he could do it. He was strong *and* fast *and* clever enough that he could outsmart us, leaving us shrieking with outraged laughter. Then we'd all get up and head to the dinner table, where Mom had a homemade meal—with "goodies," our childhood name for dessert—ready for everyone. I can still see my parents sitting at that table. Mom was tall for her generation, with good posture and poise resulting from years of ballet lessons. Just under six feet, Dad was broad and muscular. His hazel eyes contrasted with his caramel skin, and they twinkled when he told stories, especially stories about his family.

One of his favorite stories about me took place in Philadelphia when I was about four years old. Dad was doing some work on the roof of the house. Mom had sent me outside to "paint the house." Now, painting the house consisted of giving me a beach bucket filled with water and food coloring, and a paintbrush. I'd then brush the water on the house. Apparently, I was very content to "paint the house" when Daddy was working outside.

However, once I realized Daddy was on the roof, I didn't like it at all. I yelled up to him that he was going to fall and break his neck. When he didn't come down, I started marching up and down the side of the house with my paintbrush, yelling, "Daddy, you are going to fall and break your neck! Daddy, you are going to fall and break your neck!" Over and over I chanted this as only a four-year-old will do. My father became exasperated. My chanting was messing with his head. He yelled down the chimney for Mom to come bring me in the house before he really did fall and break his neck.

Ours was, in many ways, a normal, happy childhood. But outside our home, things were not so easy. My siblings and I were born alongside the Civil Rights Movement, and while my endlessly determined parents were raising their children, racial tensions boiled around us. Christmas Eve 1968 was neither the first nor the last time I would witness my parents performing incredible feats of character strength.

As an adult, I recognize that my parents' choices were guided by their shared vision of the life they wanted to provide for our family, and by the values they wanted to pass on to my siblings and me—values such as setting your own goals, making your own plan, following through on your commitments, challenging yourself to do your very best, and believing you can create your own luck. Luck in this context is having the right attitude, skills, and experience when an opportunity presents itself. Opportunities occur all the time, but you have to be able to take advantage of them. When they do, and you capitalize on them, you are positioning yourself for success and creating your own luck.

Let me expand on this. I've always believed that, no matter where your life begins, you can make yourself "luckier." My own family has been increasing our "luck" for generations—each one building upon the opportunities created by the last. My family history tells the same story over and over: Your goals don't need to be limited by where you start. Your success does not need to be dimmed by what you're born with (though of course what you're born with can help). From this perspective, anyone can increase their luck.

Here's how: in the same way my mom and dad pulled off their

"miracles"—the triumph of Christmas 1968; the budget magic that kept us all fed, clothed, and entertained, while building a college fund; the singular focus that enabled my parents to nurture a happy, healthy family in a racially charged climate. You can make yourself luckier by setting a goal, creating a plan, developing the right skills, maintaining the right attitude, and aligning your everyday choices with your goals. That's what my parents taught me to do, and that's what this book will teach you to do. It might not be easy, but it'll be worth it.

Speaking of "not easy," I faced many challenges throughout my childhood, from systemic racism to frequent moves to health challenges. Over and over again, I landed in the position of new kid, outsider, other. Each time, I had to find a way to move forward. Far from becoming barriers to my success, these obstacles became opportunities. They helped me develop strategies I would use to reach my personal goals and excel in my career. Let's talk about some of these early lessons—how I came to learn them and how they might help you.

2

Beware of Impostor Syndrome

It's sad, but it is true: Kids can be cruel to each other. Unwittingly, as children, we absorb our culture's power dynamics. Some kids take it upon themselves to reinforce these dynamics at school, while others carry the bruises of this indoctrination for years.

When I started school in Granada Hills in January 1969, just a few years had passed since the riots in the Watts neighborhood of Los Angeles, and since the Ku Klux Klan had paraded down the streets of nearby Glendale. These were local events, but the whole country was in an uproar. The Vietnam War was in full swing. Martin Luther King Jr. had been assassinated in April 1968, followed by the assassination of Robert F. Kennedy in June of the same year. I was entering first grade in a white suburb, in a racially charged city, during a turbulent time for America. You can imagine the power dynamics the school bullies would reinforce and the blows my self-esteem would take.

Research shows that little girls don't stay innocent to the ways of the world—or confident in themselves—as long as we might think. A 2017 study discovered that by the age of six, gender stereotypes are beginning to set in.[1] The same is true of racial stereotypes. Our tendency to judge people by their ethnicity increases dramatically between the ages of six and ten.[2] In these fragile years, kids take cues from their parents and teachers about social expectations, and they begin applying those expectations to the people around them and to themselves.[3]

In other words, while a five-year-old girl perceives herself as being just like any other child, a six-year-old—the age I was when I arrived in California—starts to categorize herself by gender and race. She begins to adjust her perceptions of her abilities and opportunities according to social norms. So while she might have liked math in first grade, by third grade she might say she's no good at it. If in kindergarten a girl like me can be best friends with any other child in her class, it won't be long before she finds herself gravitating toward friends who look or act more like herself.

In late-sixties Granada Hills, there were no kids who looked like me. I stood out like a sore thumb. Mom anticipated that growing up in this environment would be harder for us kids, so she got involved in organizations that directly affected us, as a way of paving the path and ensuring she had a voice to support us when needed. She would become a leader in the PTA, in the church, and in scouting. Still, many things I had to face alone, like my walk to school.

Each morning, I walked along a frontage road that paralleled the major thoroughfare, Balboa Boulevard. I'd trudge along in the dry, dusty air, carrying my little lunch box, nothing blocking my view of the station wagons and Mustang convertibles whizzing by, or their view of me.

"Hey, little nigger girl!" men would yell out their car windows. "Go back to the jungle where you belong."

When I got to school, I had "outsider" written all over me, the moment I stepped foot on campus. Right away, the teasing and harassment began—kids pointing at me and giggling, kids tripping me and pushing me down on the playground. It happened often enough that I still have scars on my knees.

But my problems didn't end with the kids. The school administration made its racism known, too. California schools had special classes for advanced students, known as the Gifted and Talented Education (GATE) program. I had always enjoyed academics, and I was particularly good at math, so when I got old enough, I took the GATE test and passed easily. I was accepted into the program. Until the school decided something had gone wrong, and the test needed to be readministered. Everyone in the program retook the test, and this time I was the only student who didn't pass.

We all know life isn't fair. "That's not fair!" is one of the early complaints children make. Instead of trying to fix situations to make them seem more fair, I was raised to accept that as a matter of truth: Life isn't fair. It never has been. It never will be. That's a fact, and you can't change it. So we couldn't use it as an excuse. When things happened, we had to figure out what we were going to do about it.

In my family, we did not complain about unfairness. In particular, we were not allowed to believe that being African American was holding us back. My parents made this choice, I would later learn, because they didn't want us to focus on the systemic racism all around us, to start finding it everywhere, and to limit our goals because of it. If we did that, they believed it really *would* hold us back. By not allowing us to use racism as an excuse, my parents hoped to empower us to overcome it. This isn't a choice parents should have to make for their children—but life isn't fair.

As a kid, I had only one explanation for why I had failed the second GATE test: I wasn't smart enough. "Too bad, Shellye," Mom said as she hugged me. "Just keep up your grades, and maybe next year you'll get in."

Many years later, Mom would admit how obvious it was that the school had made up an excuse to keep me out of the program. For Mom and Dad, the undercurrent of racial prejudice had been perceptible in Granada Hills. There were even rumors circulating in our neighborhood that Mom and Dad were Black Panthers.

However, as in any community, we met plenty of good people in Granada Hills, too. In the summer, we spent most of our free time swimming in neighbors' pools, and I became close with some of the girls in my class. Mom always got us involved in as many activities as we could handle—her way to get us out from underfoot, but also to give us as many experiences and opportunities as possible. I joined Girl Scouts as a Brownie and took ballet classes. I started to fit in and feel more at home, but still, I couldn't shake the reality that some people would never like me. It was eating away at my self-esteem. I was usually picked last for teams and left out of games, all of which I took very personally. I thought if I could just be good and nice to everyone, they would learn to appreciate me. Certain kids never came around.

A couple of years after moving to Granada Hills, I was walking home from school alone, daydreaming, swinging my lunch box in one hand, carrying books in the other, as I headed down the street that paralleled Balboa.

I sensed them before I saw them, if that's possible—two boys lunging toward me from behind a hedge. They were my classmates, boys I saw every day. They yelled something, but I hardly heard it, because I was falling backward, watching my books and my lunch box go flying, and then I felt a sharp pain as I hit the ground.

I remember this as if I am watching it happen to someone else, but it was me, lying on the sidewalk as two boys punched me and kicked me. Cars drove by in full view, but nobody stopped, and there were no adults nearby to intervene. I didn't fight back. I curled up, covering my head with my hands, and cried as they beat me. *What did I do?... Why is this happening?... Somebody help me!... Why do they hate me?...*

After a few minutes, either the boys got bored or something scared them, because they ran off. Hurting, bleeding, crying, I gathered up my books with their ripped covers. I found my thermos, which had flown out of my lunch box and broken. I packed it away, and then I walked on home.

"Hello, Shellye!" my mom yelled from the kitchen as she heard me step through the front door. Normally I would yell "I'm home!" and run into the kitchen to meet her. But today I didn't say anything.

"Shellye?" she called. "What's wrong?"

I didn't reply.

Mom walked out of the kitchen and saw the state I was in. "Shellye! What on earth?" Her face said everything as she pulled me into her arms. I began to cry again, uncontrollably, so hard I couldn't tell her what had happened for a long time.

The next day, Mom drove me to school and had a word with the principal. The two boys got in trouble, but that didn't necessarily make it any easier for me. The damage was done, and it would take a long time to repair it.

⌒

At what age do we learn to internalize cruelty? When do we start to believe it's our fault? That we deserve it? For girls, especially African American girls—and *especially* African American girls in racially charged environments—this internalization is inescapable from an early age. All the little injuries add up, and when you throw a big insult on top, it's enough to crush a young girl's self-esteem.

Early childhood experiences like these can lead to a nasty case of "impostor syndrome" later in life. Impostor syndrome is what happens when you start believing what an unjust society says about you. It is most common among girls and women, and especially women of color, but it can hit anyone who is bright and ambitious and walking into unfamiliar territory. Impostor syndrome appears as a feeling of unease, a lingering sense that you somehow don't "deserve" your own hard-earned accomplishments, that everyone else belongs except you. The effects of impostor syndrome play out in your subconscious, like a nagging, subtle doubt. It pings softly in the depths of your brain. When someone gives you a compliment, or feedback on the quality of your work—*ping!* When you get an opportunity to lead a group or get a promotion—*ping!* Whenever you feel vulnerable, or question yourself, impostor syndrome whispers, *One day, they're going to realize I'm not as great as they think I am.*

Does this sound familiar?

Unchecked impostor syndrome can severely undermine your aspirations. If you don't truly believe in yourself, it's hard to push yourself to take the calculated risks necessary to reach your goals. You might spend a lifetime building all the skills and knowledge you need to succeed, but never gain the confidence to apply them. If you don't have a safety net you can trust, within and around you, you might never find the courage to go after the educational degree, the job, or the life you really want.

No matter what bruises you sustained early in your life—be they physical or emotional—impostor syndrome doesn't need to limit you. You can learn to work with it. Here's how:

Step One: Realize you're in good company. Many accomplished people live with impostor syndrome. Its sly tendrils still sneak into my life at times, even today.

Step Two: Notice those internalized, critical, self-doubting voices when they talk to you, and understand they are not telling you the truth. Don't believe them.

Step Three: Believe the people who recognize your worth. (We'll talk about these people in chapter 3.) When people compliment you or promote you, they are doing so because you earned it. Take that at face value.

Step Four: In moments when you aren't feeling confident, rather than letting impostor syndrome take the lead, adopt a "fake it 'til you make it" mentality, projecting the confidence you want to have until it grows roots in you. I still use this trick to this day. When I attended my first Verizon board meeting, I was intimidated. Verizon was a Fortune 14 company, with CEOs of other Fortune 500 companies and global experts on the board. Yes, I was a CEO and had board experience, but for significantly smaller companies. I prepped as much as I could and spoke to sitting board members to get advice. But when it was time to go to that meeting, despite my nervousness, I put my confident face on, stood tall, and repeated the mantra in my head: "Act like you know what you are doing, listen hard, and eventually you will know what you are doing."

Step Five: It's awfully difficult to believe in yourself when you grow up in a society that doesn't expect you to amount to much, but that's your job: to overcome this obstacle and believe in yourself.

As you read on, you'll see that dismantling impostor syndrome isn't a onetime thing. I have repeated these steps many times in my life, from my preteen years throughout my career, to heal those early wounds and loosen impostor syndrome's grip on my life. We'll visit these steps again, in greater detail.

For now, if you take anything away from this chapter, take this: Life isn't fair. That's okay. Life isn't impossible, either. It's just unfair. It is not your fault that things are harder for you, but you must not let it harden you. Don't blame yourself, and don't waste your energy blaming others. If you allow life's injustices to define you, they will. But if you choose to define yourself, to believe in yourself and align yourself with others who believe in you, you will find a way to live the life you want.

3

Find Your Cheerleaders

We all need cheerleaders in life: People who, when things aren't going well, will believe in you and tell you you're a good person. People who will recognize your strengths when you can't. People who will lift you up when you don't feel capable or confident. I'm fortunate that my family members were my first cheerleaders. I know this isn't the case for everyone. If you weren't raised in a family that built you up, maybe other cheerleaders have appeared over the years—teachers, coaches, or adults in your community. One of my early cheerleaders showed up when I was nine years old.

By that time, I was the tallest kid in my class. I was growing so fast, I kept needing new clothes. Mom had a policy for this, as she did for everything: Each of us kids had a clothing budget of $200 for the year. We could either go shopping for ready-made clothing, or we could buy fabric and patterns, which were much cheaper, and Mom would do the sewing. It was a pretty clear choice, budget-wise. In the end, Mom made most of our clothes. But sometimes this meant waiting awhile, as she took care of all her other responsibilities on top of making clothes for four kids. So that summer I decided to learn how to make my own.

My sewing teacher, Mrs. Lutesinger, would have a big effect on my life and my self-esteem. One day in class, I cut a pattern wrong. I was trying to make a dress, but since I was so tall, Mrs. Lutesinger had to cut the paper pattern at the waist, then lay it on the fabric with a three-inch gap between the two pieces of the pattern, to accommodate my longer body. I dutifully pinned the paper pattern to the fabric, and then we took a break for lunch. After lunch, we returned to class to cut the fabric along the pattern lines. I forgot about the pieces being separated, and I followed the pattern right across the waistline, cutting my dress in half. Well, the other students started giggling and laughing at me. I was mortified. Mrs. Lutesinger came to the rescue. She adjusted the bottom part of the dress pattern on the fabric, making it even longer. She said we would just make a seam at the waist to fix it. Mrs. Lutesinger must have seen something in that interaction: my shyness and dismay, a piece of me that was hurting and needed help. Either way, she invited me to continue learning in her home sewing studio, one-on-one.

Mrs. Lutesinger lived way up in the Los Angeles hills, a dusty, rolling landscape carved by the wind and floods, loosely covered by barren dirt, brown grass, and pine trees. Her property sat way out on a long road, a ranch house with a big porch for looking out over the valley of suburbs. Behind the house, I was delighted to find a real, honest-to-goodness horse barn. With horses!

"Do you want to meet a horse?" Mrs. Lutesinger asked me

one afternoon. I nodded, and she led me over to a beautiful horse with a black mane and tail, and a white blaze on his face. He was the biggest animal I'd ever been close to.

She showed me how to say hello, how to stroke the horse so he wouldn't be nervous. I was nervous, though. She handed me an apple. "Here, give this to him." The horse tenderly lifted it from my outstretched palm.

She smiled. "Now, do you want to try riding him?"

Not long after, I found myself being lifted up into a saddle. The horse—I wish I could remember his name—was infinitely patient with my tense, anxious self.

"Relax," Mrs. Lutesinger told me, holding the lunge line to keep the horse steady. "I know you're nervous, but the horse can sense what you're feeling. If you're nervous, he's nervous. So you relax, and he will relax."

I willed myself to act relaxed and nonchalant. (Fake it 'til you make it, right?) I took a long, deep breath, and then we were walking. I lifted my eyes to the horizon, so far away. Suddenly I felt tall and strong, impossibly high above the world, breathing deep in the golden California afternoon. It was a moment that would change me forever.

Throughout my life, I have found my strength in moments when I am somewhat out of my comfort zone but standing on a foundation I can trust. In my childhood, my family was my foundation. Over time, I added new levels of support: skills and education, friendships, my husband and children, professional accomplishments, colleagues and mentors. When I have felt supported by something stronger and greater than myself, it has been my great pleasure and privilege to reach higher and higher, with faith that I will not fall, at least not too far. This faith—it is the opposite of impostor syndrome. Slowly, over the course of many years, connecting with people who believed in me would help me repair the damage of my experiences in Granada Hills and develop true confidence.

That afternoon, high atop Mrs. Lutesinger's horse, I felt it for the first time—a sensation of how much might be possible, with the right support. Maybe this is what Mrs. Lutesinger wanted me to feel, too. One thing I know for sure: From that afternoon onward, I was horse crazy.

I continued taking riding lessons with Mrs. Lutesinger, and I soon signed up for a group called the California Cavalry Command. We dressed in white-shirted uniforms with jaunty Western hats, and we performed complex drills with our horses. It was fun, it was hard work, and I was good at it. I don't recall cavalry being a much more diverse group of kids than my schoolmates were, but we all wore the same uniform, we had a shared activity, we acted as a team, and I felt like I fit in. Finally, I was becoming a part of something, no longer the outsider.

Around this time, another cheerleader showed up in my life: my math teacher, Mrs. Mizrahi. Despite my experiences with school bullies, I really liked school—the learning part, at least. I especially liked math, and especially competing to be the best in class. Recognizing this, Mrs. Mizrahi made a deal with me: If I could get my classwork done faster than everybody else, I could help the other kids complete theirs. This was a great motivator for me. I loved to race through as fast as I could, so I could turn around and help somebody else with their problems. It wasn't the same as being in the GATE program, but it was good for my self-esteem.

At this age, I was such a Goody Two-shoes, it hurt. Like

24

so many kids, all I wanted was for somebody to see my goodness and praise me for it. Fortunately, Mrs. Lutesinger and Mrs. Mizrahi saw my ambition and gave me opportunities to earn recognition for hard work. Their empathy kept me from becoming completely disillusioned at a fragile age, and their actions set an important example for me. To this day, I work hard to be kind and present with others, and I try to recognize that each of us carries our own burden, just as we each enjoy our own advantages.

I didn't look for my earliest cheerleaders; they found me. But once I felt the power of their influence, I knew what I had to do in every new circumstance: find the people I could cheer for and find the people who would cheer for me. From building friendships to choosing a life partner (see chapter 11), to adopting mentors and mentees (see chapter 35), to building a professional network (see chapter 36), I have spent my life knitting together personal and professional support systems and encouraging others to do the same.

Whether you're nine years old or sixty-five, the reality is that most of us aren't strong enough to face all of life's challenges on our own. At each stage in our lives and careers, we are going to need help from people who believe in us and want us to succeed. *Especially* when so much of the world just seems to want to undermine us. Yes, you can break down systemic barriers and silence the nagging doubts of impostor syndrome. Yes, you can build the life you want. But you can't do it alone. And, fortunately, you don't have to.

Who are your cheerleaders? Who believes in you when you're struggling to believe in yourself? Some people are natural cheerleaders for you. They are the ones who build your self-esteem through compliments and encouragement. If you don't have cheerleaders already, appoint someone. Seriously. Call a friend. Say, "I appoint you as my cheerleader. From now on, whenever I forget how awesome, capable, and competent I am, it's your job to remind me." Then return the favor. Together, one cheerleader to another—this is how we move forward.

4

Control What You Can

There used to be a joke among IBM families, that IBM stood for "I've Been Moved." Sure enough, after five years in Los Angeles, my dad was relocated to New Milford, Connecticut.

I was eleven at the time, so I had lived in LA almost half my life. Ultimately, I'd made some great friends there, and they threw me a going-away party. The theme was "Leaving on a Jet Plane," and that hit song by Peter, Paul and Mary was the party soundtrack. Back then, long-distance phone calls cost a lot of money, and email wasn't invented yet. So unless you were good at writing letters, when you said goodbye, it really was for good.

That farewell was difficult, but I didn't have long to grieve. I hadn't chosen this move, but here I was. So, given that life isn't fair, what could I do? As my parents had taught me to, I focused on what I could control. When we landed in Connecticut in the summer before sixth grade, Mom immediately jumped into action, and I followed suit.

The first day, Mom got all four kids together and we walked to every house in our new neighborhood to introduce ourselves. This is what we did every time we moved: We immediately put down roots. Mom joined the PTA, my sisters and I joined the Girl Scouts, my brother joined the Boy Scouts, and we found a stable where we could continue our horseback riding lessons. We spent our afternoons swimming at the lake or riding bikes along the wooded roads. Almost from the start, our days were full again.

While the girls in this new town seemed a lot like my friends in LA, the boys seemed different somehow—fascinating and impossibly cool. They wore their Adidas and Nike sneakers, blue jeans, and T-shirts emblazoned with slogans, while riding their Schwinn Sting-ray banana seat bikes. A couple such boys lived in my neighborhood, and I desperately wanted them to think I was cool, too. One early autumn day, my chance arrived. Two boys knocked on our front door. They were going for a bike ride; did I want to come?

Yes! I grabbed my coat and my bike, and I was off in a flash, pedaling fast along the winding road in the dappled sunlight. The boys hooted and yelled, and I had to work hard to keep up. Out there, the roads were perfect for young, wheeled adventurers—quiet, curvy, and steep. We soon came to a big downhill, and off the boys went, faster than light. I could barely keep up, pedaling wildly just to stay in their dust cloud. I picked up more and more speed—and then I lost control of the bike. The tires skidded out from under me, and sprawling onto the ground I went. My chin hit the gravel, and so did my hands and knees. Shocked, I immediately sprang up again, only to see blood welling up from my stinging palms.

The two boys came pedaling back, yelling, "Shellye! You okay?"

I wiped my hands on my shorts. "Oh, yeah." I grinned. "I'm fine. Let's keep going!"

Let me be clear: I was not fine. I was bruised and bleeding and shocked, but there was no way I was going to admit this to my cool new friends. So we rode farther. At first it was all I could do to try not to panic. But after a little while, I actually started to have fun again. I was getting the hang of this "fake it 'til you make it" thing. The boys were impressed by my toughness. They liked me, and as far as my eleven-year-old self was concerned, that was the important part.

By the time sixth grade began, I'd made friends in the neighborhood, at the lake, and in Scouts. Just like that, I'd become part of the community of New Milford. This new town was small, picturesquely rural, and not particularly diverse—I think there was one other African American family. Despite its homogeneity, the community seemed more tolerant and accepting (or at least less overtly hostile than Granada Hills). We were into the 1970s now, too, and the world was changing. Certainly, I didn't feel as out of place here. When school began, I hit the ground running, but not for long.

At the end of seventh grade, Dad came home with an announcement: After just two years in Connecticut, we were moving to New Jersey. Here we go again...

The funny thing is, even though they must have expected that the next relocation was always just a few short years away, my parents never acted like any place was temporary. If my siblings and I had expected to move again soon, we probably wouldn't have invested in our lives in Connecticut. We might not have felt it was worthwhile to get engaged in the community. But wherever we went, my mother led the way, and we all treated it like home, putting down roots. We didn't focus on fear of the unknown; we gave our energy to the things we could control—developing friendships, excelling in school, joining clubs and teams. I believe this attitude gave us a solid foundation, built our resilience, and taught us how to ground ourselves in the midst of change.

Like impostor syndrome, fear of change can limit your aspirations and goals, but only if you let it. As I grew into my teen years, through college, and into my career, what I learned from my mother would help me acclimate at each new step along the way: Even when you're feeling shaky and new, even if you're not sure if or how you will succeed, focus on what you can control and do the best with what you've got.

5

Don't Let Them Win

The town of Montville, New Jersey, is a bedroom community, mostly populated with professionals who commute to New York City. As usual, in this move Mom and Dad had been strategic about choosing our neighborhood, finding a modest, affordable home in the best school district. It didn't take long for us kids to realize the standard of living was higher here—the houses bigger, the cars more expensive. My siblings and I headed to school in our homemade clothes, surrounded by classmates who looked like they had stepped off the pages of a catalog, in their low-slung Wrangler bell-bottoms and platform shoes.

But the clothes weren't the worst of it. In middle school, I had started growing uncommonly fast. By the end of eighth grade, I was five foot ten, towering over friends and teachers alike. My arms and legs were stretched thin. Specifically, the ligaments in my legs became strained. Throughout the school year, I'd had a

31

lot of trouble with my knees. At first this just seemed like normal growing pains, but by the summer after eighth grade, I was in too much discomfort to play sports, and I was taking lots of ibuprofen. Concerned, my mother took me to the doctor, who told me the worst thing my thirteen-year-old self could imagine: I needed to wear braces on my legs.

Leg braces? As I enter high school?

Imagine, if you will, starting at your new high school, one of the few minority students, standing taller than most of the boys, wearing large, round-framed glasses and metal cages around your legs with hinges at the knees. Like most kids at that age, all I wanted in life was to fit in, but that would never be my luck. Worse, as the eldest of the Archambeau children, I didn't even have my siblings with me to help ease the blow. They were still in elementary and middle school. So I started alone.

I can't say starting at a new school ever became easy, and walking in with my clunky, awkward leg braces made it harder. But by high school, at least I knew the drill: Accept the circumstances, fake it 'til you make it, control what you can, and trust that things will get better. As my mother taught me to, I threw myself into everything I could—the American Field Service, French Club, and Key Club. I signed up for class projects, I volunteered for whatever opportunities came along, and I reached out to other new students, since I knew very well how they were feeling. Before long, I developed a reputation as a good student and a nice person. I even found some true, close friends, fellow ambitious students who were also a little outside the "norm" in one way or another. Just before my sophomore year of high school, the leg braces finally came off.

By then, from the outside, people saw me as a strong, solid person. But like too many teenage girls, I was still suffering from a lack of confidence. I had a necklace that I wore most days, a hollow cube on a chain. It was really just the frame of a cube, with no sides or center. I loved that symbol, because it felt like me, appearing strong on the outside but missing something on the inside. I had learned to adapt, to survive in any environment, but I worried that my strong facade was hiding my true weakness. Sometimes I felt very small.

If people knew how insecure I really am... Walking into a new environment, giving a speech to strangers, or entering an election for a leadership position in a club—each time, I'd hear this little voice in my head, questioning my capabilities. Good ol' impostor syndrome, rearing its head. Little did I know how common this is—that it takes a while to develop real confidence, to believe what your accomplishments and your cheerleaders say about you. As it was, sometimes the brave, exterior Shellye seemed like a falsehood.

At school, little incidents would prick at my insecurities. People would still "accidentally" push me into lockers, or they would pinch my butt and run away, but I had a mother who reminded me to be strong in myself. "Don't let them win," she would tell me whenever I showed signs of frustration, anger, or defeat. I know exactly where this message came from—my great-grandfather, Papa, the man who had brought his granddaughters to those lunch counter sit-ins, where they held their rightful seats, with dignity, while people tormented them, pouring milk over their heads. I pass it on to you now: No matter who tries to trip you up, stir your insecurities, or distract you from your goals, Don't. Let. Them. Win.

According to Mom, if you let someone else's actions get to you, then you're giving them control over you. In high school, she told me, "You win by staying in the game." So that's what I did. I stayed strong on the outside, and for the time being, that would have to be enough.

6

Decide What's Important to You

Mom! Can we *please* turn the heat on? It's so cold!" I made a show of shivering, wrapping my sweater tight around my thin shoulders.

Mom looked at me and raised an eyebrow. I already knew her answer.

"Well, Shellye, that depends," she said. "Do you want to go to college?"

This was not the first time we'd had this talk. I could fill in the rest: We were keeping the heat below 68 degrees because heating the house costs money, and if we could save money on heat, we could use it to pay for my college tuition.

"If you don't want the money to go to college," Mom said, "then sure, I can turn the heat up."

I understood the trade-off, but I also understood that someday, when I was an adult, I wanted to live in a warm house.

As I entered my mid-teens, I was becoming interested in what adulthood could look like. This curiosity centered on my parents and the choices they had made to provide a stable life for all of us. But before I get into that, let me say my parents could write their own books about the lessons they learned as young people. Without a doubt, their values were defined by their early experiences with adversity.

Dad's father died when he was a kid, so he was raised by his mother, who worked multiple jobs to keep the family afloat. Gran always maintained a determined, problem-solving attitude, and she always made each of her children feel loved and special. Mom was also raised by a single parent. When she was young, her mother died of leukemia. Though her dad eventually remarried, her stepmom didn't like children. As the oldest daughter, my mother shouldered much of the responsibility for caring for her two sisters. She was pushed through school at an accelerated speed, which meant she was always two years younger than her classmates, and often bullied about her size. "It made me stronger," Mom told me. "I wanted to prove to the bigger girls that I could do anything I wanted. And I did."

My parents were both problem solvers, they both wanted the best for their family, and they worked as a team to make that happen. From them, I learned what it means to have a partner in life, and how much you can accomplish when you do. Together they created a strict budget that allowed for our living expenses, college and retirement savings, and a modest allowance for each of us—but hardly a penny more. Daddy got paid twice a month, and that's when Mom went shopping. In between, if something was needed, Mom might borrow money from one of us kids' allowances, with our permission of course. We weren't broke, but our family savings were not to be dipped into. That money was held in trust for our future.

Daddy used to say Mom was a magician. He brought home his salary, and Mom turned it into a life. But as a teenager, what I saw was a woman who often seemed tired and who appeared to put everyone's needs ahead of her own, all day long. Then, after dinner, when dessert was put on the table, and after everyone grabbed for their piece, Mom always got the smallest slice of the pie *she* had made.

I was thinking about this one night, standing in our 1960s-style avocado-green kitchen, as I picked up the empty pie plate and began to scrub it. As part of kitchen duty, after cleaning, we kids were supposed to bring our parents a cup of coffee, probably as a way of letting them know we were done. So after I dried the last plate, I walked into the living room, where Mom was sitting on the green-and-gold plaid couch, knitting. I set a coffee cup on the end table beside her and declared, "Mom, I've decided. I'm not having children."

She set her work aside and cocked her head at me. "Oh? Why's that?" she asked, patting the space next to her.

I sat down. "I'm not willing to work as hard as you work and still end up with the smallest piece of pie," I said. "You never stop, you hardly sleep, and after you make dessert, you still get the smallest piece."

Mom's eyes got serious, as her hands went to her hips. "Shellye," she said, "if the pie was what I cared about, I wouldn't have the smallest piece." Then she looked deep in my eyes, smiling softly. "I have everything I care about. I don't care about that piece of pie. The key is to decide what *you* care about. You go out there and live your life and do the work to get what is important to *you*."

This critical conversation altered my worldview. Mom wasn't making sacrifices; she was making conscious choices. Just as she did with the family budget, she made trade-offs with every choice.

Around this same time, I got my first regular job, not counting babysitting. Ever since Mrs. Lutesinger's ranch, I had been taking horseback riding lessons. Lindy, Niki, and Mom took lessons, too. Then Lindy and I began to ride competitively, which required a huge time commitment on the weekends—driving out to the stables, grooming the horses, practicing, competing, and so on. Not to mention the expense. Mom came up with a rule: We had to pay for half the cost of lessons, plus reimburse Mom ten cents for any chauffeur services (a rule I grew to respect once I was a parent, by the way—recognizing the value of Mom's time). To pay my share, I picked up some odd hours feeding the horses and cleaning the stables before and after school, eventually opening and closing the barn by myself. Before long, it seemed we were spending all our free time at the stables, we loved it so much.

One day, Mom made an announcement: "Kids, I am going to buy a horse." Wait! What? We have money for a horse?

This is when I discovered that, as horse crazy as I may have been, Mom was even more so. She had always wanted a horse of her own, and unbeknownst to us, she had been saving up the money for over twelve years. The savings that weren't allowed to be touched included her horse fund. We lived below our means so we could have financial flexibility to have what was needed and desired in the future: college tuition money for us and a horse for Mom. The woman who spent her time sewing our clothes, cooking dinner from scratch, and making daily trade-offs to save money had done all of that so she could eventually have a horse. Yes, she always took the smallest piece of the pie, because she knew what she really wanted, and she went out and got it for herself. Though we were all allowed to ride Scarborough, a Thoroughbred retired from the racetrack, he was always Mom's horse, and she looked her happiest riding him.

In helping prepare me for my future, Mom didn't just *tell* me to decide what I wanted and go get it, she *showed* me how: by setting a goal, making a plan, and sticking with it, one choice, one trade-off at a time. Vision, determination, strategizing, and discipline—whether you're a teenager plotting your way to adulthood or a mid-career professional looking to make a shift, these are the cornerstones for building the life you want.

7

Set Your Goals

What do you think you want to do when you grow up?"
A guidance counselor asked me this question during my junior
year in high school.

I didn't have an answer for her.

Like most kids, I wasn't clear on what I wanted from life. I
knew what I liked: math, getting good grades, and my clubs.
But I didn't see how those things worked together. My parents'
mantra was "Work hard in school, get the best grades you can,
go to the best college, and get a good job." So that's what I'd been
doing. But what job did I want to get? I didn't know yet.

The guidance counselor tried again: "Well, what kind of life
do you want to have?"

I shrugged. "I don't know. I want to make enough money to
keep my house warm. I hate being cold."

"Okay." She smiled. "What do you like to do right now?"

Finally, something I *did* know. "Oh! Well, I like to get involved in clubs. I like all the different projects we do, and I like leading them." As I rattled off a list of my involvements, her eyes and smile widened.

"My goodness, Shellye," the counselor said. "You are ambitious, aren't you?"

"I guess so," I said. "I just like to stay involved and make an impact."

My involvement in clubs had begun with my desire to find a place for myself in my community. It continued, if I'm going to be completely honest, because of my seemingly insatiable craving for recognition. In high school, my interest in clubs leveled up when I discovered the benefits of taking on leadership responsibilities. This happened, if I can pinpoint a moment, in Girl Scouts, when I volunteered to help plan our annual camping trip and I realized that the more involved I became, the more I could influence our activities. For example, I loved hiking and I loved competitions like who could start a fire first. So I put those activities on the agenda. However, I didn't like collecting firewood—how the bugs living inside the wood would crawl out when you picked it up. So when it came time to assign chores, I put someone else's name next to that one on the responsibilities chart.

This was a revelation for me—the rewards of organizing were well worth the effort. I began applying the idea in my school clubs as well. I tested the waters when I ran for president of the French Club as a sophomore, and I won. Then it dawned on me that I might not always have to work my way into positions of power over time. Maybe I could just run for office. I started running for everything. When I joined a group, I would run for whatever roles were open: president, vice president, treasurer, whatever was on the table. Soon I had a leadership role in every group I participated in, and I loved it. It required a lot of work and a lot of coordination, but I didn't mind that. I was having a blast.

My guidance counselor picked up on that. "You know, running clubs and organizations at school isn't very different from running a business," she said. "Getting people lined up, coordinated, and working together toward a common objective—do you like that part?"

My interest was piqued. "Yes, I do like that," I said.

"In that case," she said, "you would probably like running a business."

In that moment, I knew exactly what I wanted to do in life: I, Shellye Archambeau, wanted to run a business. Initially, it didn't matter that I had no idea how I would reach that goal. All I needed to do was figure out my next best step, and my plan would unfold from there.

Of course, not all mandatory meetings with high school guidance counselors are this impactful, but I wish they were. In fact, I wish we could all meet with guidance counselors every few years throughout our lives. The questions they ask are invaluable, no matter your age: What are your goals? What aspirations and visions do you harbor that you haven't yet spoken out loud? You've got to claim them so you can go after them. This is how success begins: by setting a clear goal and committing to go after it, ambitiously, unapologetically, strategically.

PART TWO

STRATEGIZE FOR SUCCESS

8

Devise a Plan

For all the talk about "having it all" or "following your dreams," rarely do I encounter a realistic discussion about *how* to accomplish such lofty goals. Do airline pilots take off without a clear destination and flight plan? No, but that's exactly what too many people do—jump headlong into life without a strategy or even a clear set of goals. No wonder so many people find themselves grounded in the same traffic jam as everyone else, wondering what they did to get so stuck.

As I ended my junior year in high school, I had a long-term career goal. Now I needed a strategy to get me there, beginning with one big decision: where to go to college. As luck would have it, my aunt worked at Howard University, a historically black college in Washington, DC. The summer before my senior year, she helped me get a job as a secretary on campus, and I went down to DC to learn more about college life.

After growing up in the extreme minority, stepping foot on a majority African American campus was a big culture shock—in the best way. Ironically, though I looked like everyone else on the surface, I felt like a fish out of water. The students' language, the history they knew, how they interacted with each other and with me—it was overwhelming and thrilling all at once. I worked in the School of Allied Health, and I loved sitting at my desk, saying hello to the students coming and going, imagining myself as one of them. Not to mention, being around college men— who actually found me attractive and interesting—was a new experience for me. One day, a student named Marshall stopped by my desk with an invitation to go see Ashford & Simpson.

Marshall was not the first boy I'd dated; he was the second. Back in Jersey, I had briefly gone out with the only African American guy at my school. We had some fun, but he was two years older and, in our school, which was divided into "freaks," "jocks," and "nerds," he was one of the "freaks." I didn't see us having much of a future. (Yes, I was one of the "nerds," and yes, even then, even when it came to dating, I was strategizing, making decisions with an eye toward my future.) Marshall, how- ever, was perfect as my first "real" boyfriend, a college student on his way to a bright career. He was tall and kind and interesting to talk to. When I returned to high school as a senior, I officially had a long-distance boyfriend. The relationship lasted through that year, and he even escorted me to my prom, to which I wore high heels because my date (unlike most boys my age) was actually taller than I was.

Spending the summer at Howard gave me a view into college life and helped me envision myself taking my next step. When it came to choosing my own college, though, I didn't go back to the familiar. I was—you guessed it—strategic. I had researched the CEOs of the world, and I did not find many who looked like me, so I knew I needed to give myself the best head start I could get. I looked for the best schools for business, and I quickly focused in on the Wharton School, not only because it was ranked top in the country, but for economic reasons, too. Wharton's undergraduate program would prepare me for my career, so I could skip the MBA, save myself about $200,000 in the process, and get to work sooner.

Though Wharton's undergraduate program was (and is) highly selective, it was the only college I applied to, and I applied early decision. Talk about taking a risk. But I believed I had a good chance. I was a top student, I had strong SAT scores, and I had leadership and work experience.

My risk paid off. The letter arrived just before Christmas: I was headed to Wharton! So far, everything was going according to plan.

In another strategic step, I persuaded my dad to help me get a summer job. Right after graduation, I headed off to the IBM Field Engineering headquarters in Franklin Lakes, New Jersey, where my father also worked. As a relief secretary, I would be filling in for vacationing secretaries. I expected to answer phones, take messages, and do admin tasks. I didn't know it at the time, but this summer job would become a launching pad for my entire adult life.

My manager at IBM was a very practical person—by which I mean she had four pairs of shoes, all four of them the exact same style, but in black, brown, bone, and tan. I didn't realize this right away, but after a week or two it became so obvious that I had to ask.

"Gloria, you must really like those shoes," I said to her one day.

She laughed and winked at me. "Yes, I do," she said. "These are the most comfortable shoes in the world. Why would I bother wearing anything else?"

You couldn't argue with that. In fact, everything Gloria did was logical and well thought out, so when she gave me advice, I was inclined to take it.

"Shellye, you're only here for the summer," Gloria said to me as we closed up one day. "I know you're subbing in as a secretary and you have job duties to focus on, but this is also your opportunity to learn some things about business."

"Okay, how do I do that?" I asked.

"Well, this is a big office. You're going to be meeting a lot of different people. You should talk to them about what they do. Ask them how they got their job. Find out how it all works."

"Won't I be bothering them?" I asked. "They're all so busy!"

"Listen, I know this is a little intimidating," Gloria said, "but if you ask somebody nicely, you might be surprised. You're an ambitious girl, and you do have opportunities coming your way. I think anybody would feel good about having a conversation with you and giving you a little solid advice. And I'll tell you something else: People love to talk about themselves, so ask."

This sounded like fabulous advice, so I opened the company directory and started cold-calling. Probably not what Gloria had intended me to do, but it turned out to be a winning strategy. I would just look in the directory and find something that sounded interesting: *Vice President of Logistics Planning. What is that?* And I'd dial the extension.

"Hello?"

"Hello, sir, my name is Shellye Archambeau, and I'm working

for IBM this summer as a secretary. I'm going to be attending Wharton this fall, and I really want to talk to you about what you do, as I'm planning what I want to do in my career."

That was the speech I made, over and over. And do you know, the vast majority of my subjects were tickled to hear it. All summer long, I sat down with various IBM employees and found out exactly what their jobs included, what they liked about the work, what they didn't, and how they got the job in the first place. But I didn't forget why I was hired that summer. I worked hard and tried to leave the "desk" I was covering in better shape than I found it. It paid off. According to my dad, his proudest period was that summer, getting calls every week or two from IBM executives telling him what a great job I did, and how proud he should be of his daughter.

This was the beginning of a practice I've followed throughout my life: First, do the job at hand as well as you can. Second, why guess how to get from point A to point B when you can just ask somebody who's done it before? Learning this early enabled me to move successfully and quickly through my career.

If the road to success begins with choosing a goal, it continues through careful strategizing. As I'm writing this, I'm thinking about all the other choices I could have made as a young person that summer after I graduated high school. I could have taken the summer off to rest up and get ready for the changes ahead. I could have taken an easier summer job, at the stables or an ice-cream stand. I could have done the bare minimum at IBM and skated my way to payday. Honestly, none of those options occurred to me. I did what I'd been encouraged to do my whole life: I worked hard, made trade-offs, and strategized toward my goals. You can start these practices at any time in your life, or you can restart them if you've let them go. It's never too late or too early to start working toward a goal.

In the conversations I had with people at IBM, I learned a lot about planning my next steps. At Wharton, I would earn my BS in Economics. Within that degree, I would choose concentrations. Here, I operated on a piece of advice I received from an IBM executive: If you want to rise through the ranks quickly, pick a growing industry—they're expanding, they're creating more jobs, and they will offer plenty of opportunities to advance. A stagnant or failing sector, on the other hand, gets top-heavy. As companies shrink, there is more competition for the upper-level jobs, and you can get stuck.

This was the 1980s, and as I looked around, I saw one industry that was clearly poised for growth: technology. It seemed like the perfect match for my goals, and I liked math and technology just fine. Unfortunately, Wharton offered no Computer Science program at the time, so I chose Marketing and Decision Science, an analytics-based program that focused on logistics and problem-solving and that required programming courses.

When I arrived at Wharton in the fall, I had a work-study job on campus and, thanks to Mom and Dad's frugality, a fund to help pay for a good chunk of college (with a student loan and a part-time job to cover the rest). I had job experience and a clear goal. It was my time, and I was ready to take on the world. Or so I thought.

9

Learn the Ropes

Universities, corporations, government agencies—these institutions are organized power. There is so much potential held in their hierarchies, flowing through the ranks. If you can find your way in the door of a great institution, you can be a part of things that are much bigger than what you as an individual could ever achieve. That's what I've always wanted out of life: to impact things that were bigger than me. Since you're reading this book, I assume you've got ambitious goals, too.

But ambition is not just about catapulting yourself upward toward your goals. It's also about acclimating yourself at each step along the way. Whether you're entering college, starting a graduate program, beginning at a new company, or taking on a new position at a familiar company, at each new level, you need to learn the ropes and prepare yourself to excel. One of the biggest transitions young people make is the first step into college. If you're on your way to college, this chapter is especially for you. If you've already been there, you may find your own experiences reflected in these stories.

⌒

Thanks to my family's frequent moves, by the time I graduated high school, I'd had plenty of experience starting anew. So really, I was more excited than nervous about college. I was proud to have earned a spot at Wharton, and I was looking forward to living in a city after all my time in the suburbs. I was on top of the world. Or so I thought.

In truth, I had done what I needed to do to get into Wharton, but I hadn't really thought about what it meant to take on this new lifestyle socially, practically, or academically. Boy, was I in for a surprise. When I arrived on campus, I had found my way through the door of a great institution, but now I stood in the foyer, feeling simultaneously minuscule and massive. I felt big because I knew how much it had taken just to get here, small because I didn't have any role here yet, or any idea of how things worked. Overwhelmed, indeed.

My first shock came in the form of my roommate, Lisa. She was a great person, don't get me wrong, but everything about Lisa was so . . . perfect. I got my first hint of this during our pre-arrival phone call. As assigned roommates, Lisa and I had received each other's contact information from Wharton, so we spoke on the phone over the summer. Lisa's sister was already attending Wharton, so she had all the insights. Her first bit of wisdom: The dorms wouldn't have enough storage for clothes, so she was bringing a dresser to augment the small dresser they provided, and I should consider doing the same. Second, for our dorm room to look nice, we should have matching bedspreads. She would send me the information, so I could order mine, too.

Well, first of all, my mother still made most of my clothing, and I didn't have a lot of clothes, so I definitely didn't need an additional dresser. Second, my mom was going to have a fit over the bedspread. It wasn't that it was super expensive. It was just that we didn't have much disposable income in my family and—I could hear my mother's voice in my head—*Why buy a bedspread when you have a perfectly good one you can take with you?* I wasn't surprised when I ended up having to pay for that bedspread myself.

Now, in high school I'd gotten used to going to school with classmates who lived in a different tax bracket than I did, but I'd never lived with one before. Lisa came from an upper-class area of Connecticut. Her father was a senior partner in a law firm; her mother was an interior decorator. As I would learn when we finally met, Lisa was perfectly put together, from her salon-styled blond hair to her carefully applied makeup that highlighted her dark eyes. She dressed in the latest preppy fashion, and she let me know early on that she didn't share clothes.

Despite our different upbringings, it's fair to say Lisa and I both were in for big learning experiences. As we moved through the school year, shedding old assumptions and integrating new ideas, we became close friends. My point is this: Anytime you enter a new situation, you might feel out of place, but you're not alone. Even if other people look like they belong, most everyone feels out of place in new situations. More importantly, that feeling is temporary. Be patient with yourself and trust that you'll find your way.

The city of Philadelphia and the UPenn campus, where the Wharton School is housed, offered many opportunities for exploration. They were full of interesting, brilliant, and compelling people in all colors and shapes. Though our campus was predominantly white, given the size of the school, there were a lot more of everybody. Instead of being one of two or three black people in my class, now I was among hundreds of other African Americans and people of other ethnicities. I had access to an entire community I'd never before had an opportunity to join. In many ways, I was still quite naïve, despite my two months at Howard University. I was surprised by how little I knew about African American culture. People would use slang and phrases I didn't understand. I was introduced to new music and dance moves. Even the popular card games of bid whist and Spades were different from what I had played in high school. Most importantly, though, I learned that African American identity wasn't really about those things. It was about having a shared history of living in and experiencing America as a black person.

At times, my social learning curve felt steep, but that was nothing compared to academics. At Wharton, I quickly learned that I wasn't as smart as I thought—or, more accurately, that I needed to get a lot better at studying. I had always done well in school, but my biggest secret weapon was cramming. Juggling school, work, and extracurriculars, I had mastered the technique of learning everything right before the test. I paid attention in class, took notes, and the night before a test, I'd study like crazy. Well, that didn't work so well in college, where the classes covered so much more material, and typically there were only two exams during a semester. After my first midterms, I had two Bs and two Cs. I was mortified. To make matters worse, every single person at Wharton was as competitive as I was, and many of them much more so. These were some of the best and brightest students in the country, and we were all getting graded on a curve. Clearly, I had a lot of learning to do here at college. Eventually I would see that I didn't need to do all of that learning alone.

Let me jump ahead for a moment, to the first semester of my sophomore year. By then, I had developed some new study skills, and I was doing fairly well in my classes, but Accounting was kicking my butt. In that class, I got my first D on an exam, my first D ever in my life. I thought I would die. I was so ashamed. As far as I was concerned, a B was a shortfall. I was depressed about it for days before my internal voice finally broke through: *So, what am I going to do about it?* I went to see the professor. He pointed out that I had spent too much time creating the required balance sheet, so I had run out of time for the rest of the exam. The professor gave me two tips for studying and suggested sections of the text to concentrate on next time. By making that visit, I had shown my professor that I cared about my performance and that I was focused on improving. I clawed my way back to a C in the class, but the real lesson was this: When you need help, ask for it. I wish someone had told me that before I began college, which is why I'm telling you now. Don't struggle in silence. Go talk to your professors. (The same advice applies in your career, but we'll get into that later.)

Okay, back to freshman year. Encountering new people, a new home, new ideas, new responsibilities, new freedoms, new food, new opportunities—my first semester at Wharton spun me. I didn't realize quite how much, though, until November rolled around, and I found myself getting a bit moody. I knew

I missed my family. I hadn't been home yet, and because long-distance calls were expensive at the time, I couldn't call home unless it was an emergency. So I didn't even have phone contact to help ease the transition. But it wasn't until I went home for Thanksgiving that I figured out what I was missing most: hugs. My family is a "touchy" family. We hug, pat, clasp hands. I didn't get any of that at Wharton, and I longed for it. That, and Mom's cooking. Mom was an excellent cook, and Wharton's cafeteria food was average at best. Let's just say, I never gained the dreaded "freshman fifteen." As a matter of fact, I lost some weight.

Looking back, I don't know if anything could have prepared me—or could fully prepare any young person—for the transition to college. Stepping completely out of your element, in every single facet of your life, all at the same time? How do you get ready for that? My parents had encouraged me to get the best education available, to increase my opportunities to support my-self as an adult. But when you're a kid, the idea of "opportunities" is a vague one. It really isn't until you step out on your own that the full, dizzying reality of opportunity becomes visible. Eventu-ally, what helped me adjust to Wharton was the same thing that had helped me make transitions as a kid: getting involved in activities and finding friends.

By the end of freshman year, I had joined several groups— Wharton Women, Stepping Stones, and the gospel choir—and I found my people there. In an effort to connect more deeply with the black community on campus, for sophomore year I made plans with my friend Carla to move into the W.E.B. Du Bois College House, a dorm community centered on African Ameri-can culture, with a calendar of enrichment and social activities. I also joined Black Wharton, an organization that focused on business and leadership. I made sure to develop friendships in all the groups I traveled between, but this was the first time I was part of an African American social scene, and I loved everything about it. I learned more about African American history, and I had the chance to meet and hear community leaders like Jesse Jackson. Quite a few of the people I met through Black Wharton also had grown up in predominantly white environments. Finally, I had friends with shared experiences. We could empathize with each other's situations and stories. For once, I wasn't the only one in the room.

As I developed friendships at Wharton, the spin of my first year began to stabilize, and I learned for myself what recent research has proven: The connections you make in college can actually help you perform better.[4] Far from getting in the way or distracting you, your social circles can enhance your progress. If you think about it, it makes sense that the people who do best in college are the ones who have several circles of friends, one for every environment. The friendships you develop in college differ from your earlier relationships. These are your first real colleagues. You connect because you like each other, yes, but you also depend on each other as teammates, or as study partners, or classmates who'll share resources or lend lecture notes, or even as fill-ins for your family. For minority college students in particular, tight circles of friends become safe spaces that offer support, comfort, and acceptance, and this improves student confidence and performance.

As an adult looking back, I understand that when my parents talked about the opportunities college would bring, this is what they meant: the chance to see what I might be able to accomplish, to develop my skills, experience, and connections, so I would be ready to take bold steps toward my goals. In that way, a college education is so much more than the sum of its academic parts. It's the feeling that you belong to something, you have a foundation of excellence, you have professors to advise you, you have people to call on if you need them, and you have people who can call on you. As I closed my first year of college, I was no longer overwhelmed in the foyer of the institution. I had learned the ropes. I had found my people. Now I was steadily walking the halls.

Even better, I had identified a common pattern that plays out in the lives of ambitious people: Every time you take a giant leap forward, you will land at the bottom of your next learning curve. That's okay. That's just how it goes. You might not know everything you need to know yet, but you can trust your ability to learn the ropes.

10

Prepare for Opportunity to Appear

Okay, what I'm about to tell you might sound crazy. At least, to my sophomore-year roommate, Carla, it did.

One Saturday during fall semester, I went shopping at an outlet mall for a winter coat. This was 1981, so the style was all about big shoulder pads, baggy sleeves, and a tight, belted waist. Regardless, I picked out an A-line, double-breasted, wool swing coat.

"What do you think?" I asked Carla when I returned, doing a little catalog-inspired pose.

Carla's face scrunched up. "I don't know, Shellye," she said. "Don't you think that's a little out of style?"

"Yeah," I said, "but it will still fit me when I get pregnant, right?"

Carla's eyebrows pushed lower. "Pregnant? You don't even have a steady boyfriend!"

"Okay, but hear me out. I'm nineteen right now, and I want to get married and have kids young, so I expect to be pregnant in five or six years. A coat I buy now should last that long, so why should I have to buy a new one when I'm pregnant?"

Carla scoffed. "I don't know, how about to look good?"

"No, seriously! Listen, if I get this coat now, every time I wear it, I'm going to be thinking about the future. But if I get a different coat, I'm just going to be thinking about how I look in it right now. Like, I'll be breaking my promise to myself by not planning for my goal."

"Sure, Shellye," Carla said, "I get it. You can plan all you want to get pregnant at twenty-five, and you can buy the coat to match, but tell me, where's the man going to come from?"

"I don't know," I said. "But at least I know where the coat is coming from."

Yes, at nineteen years old, I bought a coat that could double as maternity wear. Hey, I was raised by a woman who, on a shoe-string budget, somehow managed to buy a Thoroughbred horse. I knew that little choices and trade-offs led to big rewards. To that end, during sophomore year I also began volunteering to work on the catering crew for campus events, having learned that after the guests left, I could bring home leftover trays of cheese and hors d'oeuvres. Every meal I could get for free meant a few more dollars in my savings account. In this and many other ways, I was always strategizing, always planning for the future.

The American Dream is not easy to attain. It can take gener-ations, as it did in my family, for a person to feel like they've "made it." Thanks to the generations before mine, I started off in a pretty good place, but I still couldn't afford to take anything for granted. Fortunately, my parents had gifted me with the ability to plan my way toward the life I wanted, and by example, they taught me the degree of discipline it takes to support my plan. At a young age, I learned that success is about preparing for opportunities to appear, so you are ready to take advantage of them when they do. In that way, as I like to say, you can make your own luck.

However, not everyone feels this sense of agency.

In the wake of the Great Recession of 2008, many young people lost hope in the American Dream. Where my generation believed we had the power to shape our own lives, young people today say they see success as something that's mostly reserved for the fortunate.[5] That makes me sadder than I can say. Yet I understand why people might feel this way. Just take a look at economics. Today, only twenty of the fifty states in the United States require that schools teach students the basics of financial and economic literacy,[6] which means most young people aren't getting the education they need to make wise financial choices early in their lives. (Luckily, we have the internet now, and a quick Google search will lead you to the financial advice you need.)

On top of that, today's college graduates are under greater financial strain than preceding generations, yoked with school loans and credit card debt as they attempt to launch their careers and grow their families. Worse, it's been well documented that women work harder for less money, rendering them less financially secure than men, not just in the US but around the world.[7] It's more difficult (though, of course, not impossible) for women to accumulate wealth, to maintain good credit, to plan for the future, to secure their own retirement. Not to mention the very real forces of inequality that still act as roadblocks to so many Americans.

If you're feeling any of these pressures, believe me, I understand. It's not your fault you're standing where you are, but it *is* possible for you to change your circumstances. You have to believe that: You have the power to create change. I know this because I know my grandmother's story. When her husband died, she became a single African American mother without a college education, and every day was a struggle. It doesn't matter how well you can balance a checkbook if nobody will give you a paycheck. Still, she did eventually get a job, actually more than one, and she applied every ounce of skill she had to keeping her family afloat. This is the environment my father came from, and it's the knowledge he passed on to his children: No matter your circumstances, you have the power to advance in your life.

Yes, it took my family many generations to achieve the American Dream, for reasons that are painfully obvious—as the manumission deed in my family archives attests, I am a descendant of slaves. But with time, hard work, and strategic choices, we have arrived at a place where we can offer our children a sound economic footing. Maybe we had to work harder than some other families to get here, but we got here. I want that same comfort for everyone.

But progress doesn't happen by accident. You need a goal, you need a plan, and you need to maximize every opportunity you encounter. After all, what use is a dream if you have no strategy for making it come true? What's the value of visualizing the heights you'll climb to, if you lack the tools to build a ladder? For me, in college, maximizing opportunities meant choosing a practical coat over the fashion of the day, it meant volunteering in exchange for a shot at the leftovers, it meant keeping my eyes on the future while doing everything I could to prepare for success today.

11

Strategic on All Fronts

As sophomore year closed and summer break arrived, I decided to move off campus with a group of friends, renting a house on Spruce Street. From the minute we moved in, that place was full of life. We housemates would cook together and share our stories of the day with each other, like a family. We had friends coming and going all the time. One Saturday, one of my housemates suggested we get some wine and cheese and have a picnic on the flat section of our roof, so we did. I felt so grown up. Little did I know I was about to make one of the most important decisions of my adult life. But first let me give you some background.

For the past year, I'd had an internship at IBM. It was a big place where you could meet all different types of people, and it seemed like there was always some kind of party happening on Friday evenings. Anytime someone was getting promoted, having a baby, having a birthday—any reason to celebrate at all—people would pool their money and rent out a boathouse on the river. When school was in session, I didn't have time to socialize with people from work, but the summer was different.

"Are you going to the boathouse party?" a fellow intern asked me one Friday in June.

"I wish," I said. "I don't have any way to get there."

"Well, that's no problem, I'll drive you," she said. "Come on, you'll love it."

Why not? I hopped in her car after work.

A boathouse party sounded incredibly fancy to me, but when we arrived, I saw it was just a laid-back gathering—everyone talking and dancing in that early summer glow. I love to dance, so that's what I did to soothe my nerves. I felt very sophisticated, dancing with my older coworkers. One man in particular asked me to dance a few times, always during a fast song, but it seemed like every time we started dancing, the music would change to a ballad.

"Don't we have funny luck," he said, laughing, after it happened the second or third time. His eyes twinkled. What a nice guy, and good-looking, too, in his suit and tie. He was built like an athlete, six foot two with broad shoulders and a slim waist. He carried himself with confidence and an air of fun, not to mention he was making me feel right at home with his easy banter, even though I was younger than almost everybody. He was older than me, too, probably around thirty-five.

I danced with that guy a few more times, and he introduced himself as Scotty, from Sales. He seemed to be flirting, given how many times he'd ask me to dance. As far as I was concerned, he was too old, and I wasn't interested. But we were having fun, and we were among coworkers, so I just kept dancing.

Around ten o'clock, the party started breaking up. People on the dance floor were talking about an after-party at a club called Whispers.

"Are you going to the after-party?" I asked my friend.

"No, I have to get back," she said. "Can you get a ride?"

"I can give you a ride there," Scotty said. Funny how he was still nearby. "What do you say? I can drive you home afterward."

I looked at him and thought about it for a second. He was a stranger, but not that strange; we worked together at the same office, after all. All our coworkers would be there. It wasn't like I was heading out to a bar with some random guy. What could go wrong?

"Okay," I said. "Let's go to Whispers."

Scotty drove me there in his black Mazda RX-7. He opened the car door and the club door for me, which I thought was sweet, and he bought me a drink while we waited for our coworkers. Then we hit the dance floor again.

After a couple of songs, I looked around. "Scotty," I said, "do you see anybody from the party here?"

He shook his head. "They'll show up. I guess they're just taking their time."

Not one of our coworkers ever showed up. I had personally talked to half a dozen people who were planning to meet us at Whispers, but it never did happen.

So there I was, dancing with a man almost twice my age, late into the night. And frankly, having a wonderful time. We talked about events of the day, including the appointment of Sandra Day O'Connor to the Supreme Court. He told me the world would be a better place if women ran it. He had a great sense of humor, and he entertained me with stories about IBM customers and his family.

When Scotty drove me home that evening, I knew he wanted to see me again. I'll admit by this time I was becoming interested, too. He was kind and handsome, but though he seemed much younger than his age, the age was a real problem. So when he walked me to my door and said, "I'd love to see you again," I looked him straight in the face.

"Scotty, how old are you?" I asked.

He smiled sheepishly. "I'm thirty-eight," he said.

"Well, I'm nineteen. I'm sorry, Scotty, you're too old for me, but thank you. I had a really great time."

"Wait, what are you talking about?" he said, opening his hands wide. "Why—"

"No," I said. "Thank you, but no." I turned and walked through my front door, closing it in his face.

After that night, I started running into Scotty everywhere at work. Funny, we worked in different buildings, and I'd rarely seen him before, but there he was, walking through the bullpen toward my desk, strolling through the demo room where I trained on the machines, and hanging out at the building entrance as I headed out at the end of the day. He seemed to be everywhere, and every time I saw him, I wanted to see him again. I tried to talk myself out of it, this infatuation. It was silly. But pretty soon I found myself looking for Scotty, hoping he'd walk around a corner and smile at me again.

Okay, Shellye, I said to myself after a few weeks of this. *You need to get this out of your system. Go on a date with this guy, find out what's wrong with him, and get over it.*

I don't know what I expected, but dating an older man was

definitely different from going out with younger guys. Gone were the bravado and false charm of a young guy who just wanted a good-looking girl, and in its place were Scotty's self-assurance and humility, his dry wit and what seemed to be a sincere interest in me. Instead of spending our time together telling me about himself—his day, his interests, his opinions—he seemed to have an insatiable curiosity about me. He actively listened. He treated me like a person, and above all, he treated me with a little more honor and respect than I was used to getting.

We went on one date, and another, and another. We both loved dancing, and I think we both felt a little awkward about this May-December thing, so we went back to Whispers quite often. Dancing always broke down the awkwardness and returned us to a more natural interaction. When we stopped being so self-conscious about our age difference, we had an easy repartee. He took me to modest dinners and free concerts. I wouldn't let him spend a lot of money on me, because I didn't want the experiences that money could buy to cloud my thinking. But whatever we did and wherever we went, it seemed we were far away from my college experiences. I could see myself as a grown woman and try on that life. It was like stepping into a future I'd previously only imagined.

On paper, this shouldn't work, but it was working. I started to wonder if I was even in control of the situation. I really liked this guy, and he really liked me.

By the way, Scotty eventually admitted that, back at the boathouse party, the DJ had been his nephew. Scotty was giving him the sign to slow down the music whenever we danced. Then his good friend Ed went around telling people there was a change of plans for the after-party—and they all went to a different club. I was set up. Turns out I'm not the only one who puts plans in place to get what they want.

⌒

One day in July, I was reading in my room when I heard voices in the hallway, a couple of my roommates. "Gosh, he's just so old," one of them said.

I froze. They had to be talking about me and Scotty. I cocked my ear toward the door, and sure enough, it was all about me and my weird older boyfriend.

I had a choice: hide in my room and act like I wasn't home, or open the door and confront them. I decided on the direct approach. I stepped into the hallway. This time, my roommates froze, looking at me with their jaws dropped open. I almost laughed to see their embarrassed faces. Instead, I smiled. "Hey," I said. "Listen, it's an old house. The walls are thin."

Nervous chuckles.

"It's all right, you guys," I continued. "Scotty *is* old."

We all had a little laugh at that fact. Crisis averted, but I knew I was in bigger trouble than simply a bit of roommate gossip. I'd just turned twenty years old. Scotty was eight years younger than my dad and eighteen years older than me. How in the hell was this going to work? What would my family say? This was going to be a challenge, and I had to decide if the challenge would be worth it. Was Scotty someone I wanted to get serious about?

I believe that people come as a package, a combination of great qualities and not-so-great qualities. No one is perfect, so in choosing a life partner, you have to know what you absolutely need in a partner and what you can live without. I set out to do this work for myself. First, I wrote down the qualities I was look-ing for in the ideal guy—handwritten, on graph paper, for my eyes only. I put a lot of thought into what I wanted, and I came up with a long list initially. Then I scrutinized it and eliminated everything that wasn't truly critical. My final list included qual-ities like self-confident; self-sufficient; can cook, clean, and do laundry; fun, likes people; family oriented; willing to stay home with the kids; supports me and loves me unconditionally.

Now all I had to do was find out which of the things on this list Scotty didn't have; then I'd have a reason to call off the relationship.

At the end of each date, Scotty would park his car in front of my house and turn it off. We'd stay in the car for hours and just talk and talk and talk some more. About everything. Mostly, I was asking him questions, and not easy ones. I grilled him on his philosophy, his personality, his goals in life. I was really, truly pushing to find a reason, any reason, why I shouldn't marry this guy. Because that's what I wanted: to get married soon and have kids young. After that, I wanted to achieve great things in my career. I needed to know that this thirty-eight-year-old man was ready to support my vision. If he wasn't, then I needed to move on and find somebody else who was.

That's how it went for me in college: When I was dating someone, if I determined he wasn't marriage material, I stopped dating him immediately. After all, I wanted to increase my odds of getting married in my early twenties, and staying committed to someone just for fun would reduce my opportunities to meet my right life partner. For his part, Scotty felt his own urgency. He knew our age difference was a problem. Plus, he had been married before, and he didn't want to get into anything that wasn't going to make him happier than being single. So we talked, on and on, evening after evening, under the streetlamp in front of my old row house on Spruce Street.

It didn't take long for me to find the skeletons in Scotty's closet, and you can believe I unpacked each one and held it up to the light. I found out he'd been wild. In college, he liked to party, and he seemed to be in the middle of controversy often. As a matter of fact, Morgan State University had tried to throw him out of school a couple of times. But in addition to his antics, he was a strong student and athlete and always managed to talk his way out of situations. Even later, after being drafted into the army as an MP, Scotty was a work-hard, party-hard guy. He told me all about his loan sharking days, lending other guys money until payday and charging them double at payback time. He even told me about a major mishap he'd never been caught for (and one I'd better not detail here) that could have landed him in serious trouble. Instead of getting caught, he got his honorable discharge and went into the working world, mostly unscathed.

I was glad Scotty was sharing with me, but as a confirmed Goody Two-shoes, I found his history alarming. Add to that the fact that he'd already been married and it hadn't lasted. Since then, he'd been single and hadn't planned to get married again.

"I just never met anybody who seemed like marriage material before," he explained. "Not that I'm against it, I just haven't wanted to."

"But you love your family, you love kids," I said. "Don't you want that in your life?"

He smiled at me, his eyes twinkling. "With the right person, yes."

I had to think about it myself. *What would a life be like with this man? What kind of a husband would he be?* I decided to ask my mom's advice on what to do next, what else I needed to find out about this guy.

"Well, you ought to find out how he treats his own mother," she said. "I've always believed a man will ultimately treat his wife like he treats his mother."

So I asked and I watched, and I found out Scotty was a fantastic son. He'd given his mother and sister financial help at various times of need, and he'd even taken them on a trip to Europe. "I go visit Mom now and then," he said. "Just to check and see how she's doing. I'm her favorite." Sure enough, I could see the strength of their relationship when they were together.

When I reported this back to my mother, she got quiet for a minute. Then she said, "Shellye, what are you going to do when he asks you to marry him?"

"Mom! It's only been a few months. Nobody's getting married yet," I said. But my stomach was full of butterflies.

"Well, you should be ready," she said. "Sounds to me like he is."

Now, I realize my dating strategy might sound a bit over the top. I also realize not everyone wants to get married or wants to have children at such a young age. We've come a long way since the days when I was vetting Scotty as a potential life partner. Dating is different. Marriage is different.[8] Families are different. People are making different life choices. More people are choosing not to have children, and those who do choose to have kids are having them much later, having fewer of them, and raising them differently.[9] Your relationship choices and your family might look very different from mine. But no matter what you want, you can set your life up to increase the odds of making

71

it happen. If finding a life partner is on your list, the approach I used in college still works: Decide what you want, determine what you need, and strategize from there. Talk about everything, share your expectations and plans, and find someone who is on the same page as you.

⌒

It was August, and the hot nights of dancing and muggy conversations in the Mazda were still as refreshing to me as a walk among the stars. I was over my head now, and my heart knew desperately what it wanted. But there was something Scotty and I hadn't talked about, and I was running out of time to bring it up. If Scotty was getting ready to propose, I had to ask him my big question.

"Scotty," I said to him one evening, there in the driveway in the blue Philadelphia night, "I know we've talked about kids. You want kids, and I want kids, too."

"Yes, that's right," he said.

"Well," I said, "when I was growing up, Mom was always home. I'd come home from school, and Mom was there."

"Mine worked off-shifts," Scotty shared, "so she could be home with us when I was little."

"So when I got home, I was always the first one back from school. I'd run in the door, drop my books, and the first thing I'd do is get a snack. Mom would keep me company and ask about my day. And then I'd go off and do my homework or whatever, and roughly the same scenario played out when my sisters and brother got home. Then we all ate dinner together once Dad got back from work."

Scotty smiled. "Okay…"

"Well, when Dad came home, I remember we never had much to tell him about our day. Because we had already shared everything with Mom. It was like, that was old news. But Mom knew everything about our lives, because she was there right when we got home. She had to prompt us to tell Dad about things that happened."

Scotty nodded and raised an eyebrow at me.

"So I decided," I said, "I would really like to be able to have someone stay home with the kids, especially when they are in school."

"Oh yeah." He smiled. "That would be a nice thing."

"Yeah," I said. "But the thing is…I just don't want it to be me." And I gave him a look.

Scotty paused, eyes a little wide as the realization dawned on him. "Huh," he said.

I looked at him carefully, and I stayed quiet, watching him think it through.

After a while, Scotty sighed. "You know, Archambeau," he said, "I've had a lot of experiences in my life. I've had three different careers, and you know I like working."

I held my breath.

"But," he said, "I think I could see myself doing that, for you."

I smiled. "Okay then." In that moment, I knew for sure. This was the man for me.

⌒

A couple weeks later, Scotty picked me up for a date. We were going back to Whispers, our favorite club, to go dancing. He pulled into a parking spot and turned the car off, and I started to open my door—but Scotty leaned back in his seat.

Hmmm, I thought. I took my hand off the door.

Scotty turned on the car stereo. Earth, Wind & Fire's "Let's Groove" played softly. Scotty sighed and gave me a deep look. "Hey, Archambeau," he said, "do you want to get married?"

Time slowed down, or maybe it stopped. Deep down inside me, I heard a quiet little voice: *Okay, Shellye. This is it. Are you sure this is what you want? Are you ready to jump off this ledge into the unknown?*

But it wasn't unknown. I had planned for this. I knew this man. I'd found out everything I could about him. I knew he would be a good partner and a cheerleader when I needed one. He knew what I wanted from life, and he was willing to support me in it. He was good to his family, and I believed he would be a good father. I knew I wanted to get married and start a family young. In fact, I couldn't wait. And yes, I could see a life with Scotty. We'd already talked about it so much I could picture it happening. We'd talked about it so much he almost didn't have to propose. *But he's proposing like this?* I thought. *It's so sudden, so casual. Do I care?*

Mom was right, she told me he was getting ready to ask me. She told me to think about what I would say. I did think about it. I knew what I was going to say. I smiled ear to ear. "Yes."

And then we kissed, and then we went dancing.

12

Foster Self-Determination

Before I tell you how my family responded to my engagement to Scotty, I want to pause for a moment and talk about self-assurance.

Self-assurance is the ability to say yes to yourself when most people around you are saying no. It's the power of believing in your own ability to make choices about your life—and not just to make choices, but to make them responsibly.

As a young person, I didn't come by self-assurance easily. Or maybe I could say I was born with a certain self-assurance but I nearly lost it during my schoolgirl years in Granada Hills. Confident little-girl Shellye, who had taken charge when her sisters were worried about Santa, in many ways faded into the walls for a while. It took me over a decade—from age eight to eighteen or so—to grow my sense of self, to fill in the cube pendant I wore on my necklace in high school.

During that time, I was lucky to be surrounded by a loving family and to encounter some attentive teachers. Whether due to nature or nurture or a combination of both, I continually pushed myself to live up to my potential, and I stepped up for challenging opportunities that would coax me out of the shadows. As I grew into my own skin, I discovered over and over that my potential was greater than I expected.

As I now understand it, we become self-determined people when we are fulfilled in three psychological areas: competence, autonomy, and relatedness.[10] In a nutshell, competence is the ability to handle yourself; autonomy is the sense that you can make your own choices and look out for your interests; and relatedness means feeling like you fit in. Research shows that if you don't have all three, you'll be more likely to struggle or withdraw from challenges. But if you do manage to strengthen all of them, you will be prepared to set your own life goals and reach them.

Looking back, I see how carefully my parents steered me toward developing all three categories. Though this research didn't exist at the time, their instincts and life experiences gave them plenty of wisdom. Today, when I look around at my successful colleagues, mentors, and heroes, I see that they, too, work on these qualities, constantly filling those wells so they are able to continue drawing from them. It seems that, once you develop the right combination of relatedness, autonomy, and competence, you tend to know how to maintain it.

When I reflect on my own self-determination, I see that I grew up with relatively high levels of competence and autonomy, but my sense of relatedness was not as well developed. Though I worked hard to make connections with people, as the "only" or one of few minorities, I still felt different. This is why, when I finally arrived at Wharton, I would seek out other African American students. I wanted to develop friendships with people whose life experiences were similar to mine. Increasing my relatedness would help me while I was adjusting to college life, and it would continue to pay off in the long term.

Without a doubt, young women, people of color, immigrants or children of immigrants, people with disabilities, LGBTQ youth, first-generation college students—anyone growing up "different"—will face more challenges on the path to true self-determination. But I believe anyone, at any stage of life, can build a better foundation.

Take a look at your own life. Which key factors of self-determination have you developed? Which are lacking? What could you do to develop your competence, autonomy, and relatedness? Even small steps can make a big difference—like calling on executives at IBM to learn about their jobs (competence), like learning how to sew instead of waiting for Mom to make my clothes (autonomy), like developing connections with new classmates in college (relatedness). What small steps can you take to develop your self-determination? Taking them now will strengthen your ability to set and reach your ambitious goals.

It will also strengthen your ability to stand firm in your decisions, even when others aren't so sure.

13

Take a Stand

I started dating Scotty in June, and we were engaged in September. I finished my sophomore year at Wharton as a single woman, and at the start of my junior year, I was a fiancée. The whirlwind romance was exciting and a little scary, but at the same time it just felt *right*. I didn't feel I was jumping into anything. I'd done my homework. I'd done my research. I felt prepared and fully aware of what I was doing.

However, not everyone felt the same confidence.

When I called Mom and told her that Scotty had popped the question, her response was deadpan: "And you said...?"

"I said yes, Mom. We're engaged!"

"Well, Shellye, congratulations! I'm happy for you," my mother replied, her deadpan tossed to the wind. "I always knew you would marry somebody older. You've always been an old soul. I used to tell people you were three going on thirty."

I laughed, still full of butterflies. "Thanks, Mom."

"But listen, eighteen years is a big difference," she went on. "I just want to be sure you've thought about what that's going to be like for you. Not now, not today, but in thirty or forty years. The big issues aren't now, they are later. When he is in his seventies and you are in your fifties. You will be in two different stages, physically, possibly health-wise. Just make sure you're looking at this with your eyes wide open."

"Yes, Mom," I said. "I am. I thought about it when I was wondering if he was the right guy for me, and I thought about it again when you told me he was going to propose. I know what it means, but I know he's the right person for me."

"Well then, I am in full support," she said. "So how do you want to tell your father and your brother and sisters?"

"Do you think you could keep it between us for now?" I asked. "Maybe I can come home and tell them in person."

"I think that's a good idea," she said softly.

Dad was a tougher nut to crack. Or perhaps a tougher book to read. For all his charm and his skill at telling stories, he is not one to talk about his own feelings. So I came home on a weekend and took him to lunch, and I told him, and he congratulated me kindly. But I really had no idea how he felt about it. Later, Mom told me he was worried about the age difference. "But he trusts your judgment, Shellye," she said. "He trusts you to make this choice."

My sisters Lindy and Niki, at this time, were eighteen and seventeen, respectively. Arch was only fifteen. Lindy was just getting ready to go off to college, and Arch couldn't even drive yet. Though I was twenty now and growing into my adulthood, to them I was still their peer, and they were not impressed by my pushing-forty fiancé.

79

"Really," Niki said when I told them, her skepticism like a cold breeze. "Okay...I'm happy for you, I think."

"Yeah, congratulations," Arch said with a half smile.

Lindy had no words at all. She honestly did not like Scotty, who had teased her a little too much the first few times they met. She didn't approve of this rude man, and she didn't care if I knew it.

And then came my grandmother. A week or two later, I went to visit Gran, and I wasn't in her house ten minutes before she started in on me. "Shellye, that ring on your finger comes off as easy as it went on," she said with a stern look.

"I know, Gran," I said. "I've thought about that."

"Well, have you thought about why he never married again after his first wife? Now he's thirty-eight. What was he doing all those years? Do you think—"

"Gran," I cut her off. "I love you. But if this is all we're going to talk about this weekend, I'm going back to campus. I'm here to visit you, and I hope you can be happy for me, but I've made my decision, and no matter what you say, I'm not going to change it."

Gran looked at me sharply. And then she changed the subject.

Eventually, my whole family would come to love and accept Scotty. But in those early days, they gave me many opportunities to practice a skill I would use time and again throughout my life: expressing confidence in my well-reasoned decision, even in the face of skepticism. I knew what I wanted, and I stood up for it, and eventually they fell in line with me.

14

Build Your Reputation

I entered my junior year at Wharton with my custom-built life plan in full swing. I was newly engaged, working three days a week at IBM, taking a full load of courses, participating in various social organizations, and still volunteering to work at receptions so I could bring home the free cheese platter. Can I say my life was a whirlwind? But I loved it.

That year, I hit my stride as a college student. I knew how things worked, and my old tendencies toward leadership returned. Junior year, I ran for president of Black Wharton, and I won. I started gravitating toward organizational roles in class projects and clubs. I was getting better at recognizing my teammates' unique skills and interests, and I enjoyed planning projects that made everybody feel motivated and proud of the outcome.

Personally, my big goal was to graduate in good standing and with a wedding fund (that's why I was still taking leftover cheese platters). Scotty and I had already agreed there was no reason to get married until after I graduated, so our four-month courtship was followed by a nearly two-year engagement. We saw each other on weekends when we could. Meanwhile, I was saving money just as aggressively as ever. Already I had a few thousand dollars in the bank, but I wanted at least ten thousand.

Without a doubt, I was overextending myself, but I was energetic and enthusiastic about it all. I couldn't bring myself to let anything drop, so I learned to survive with less sleep. It wasn't easy. I mean, I had moments when I neglected my relationship with Scotty a little too much as I focused on my college life. At times, my schoolwork suffered because I was so busy. Occasionally the stress caught up with me, and I completely freaked out, letting doubts and negativity fill my head, convincing me I was going to fail at all of it. Then I'd remember to call my friends or my mother to calm me down. But mostly, I was managing to keep everything afloat.

That year flew by so fast I practically got whiplash. It was not until the first week of my senior year that I paused momentarily to assess my progress. That week, I started a new marketing class where we would complete consulting projects for real companies. The professor divided us up into our working groups, and I started by saying hello to everybody, introducing myself as I usually did.

One of the girls said, "Shellye, I'm excited to work so closely with you. You've got such a great reputation!"

I was a little surprised. I knew this student by sight, but we had never met. I didn't think of myself as a high-profile student on campus, and I didn't know about any reputation, or how she had heard about it. Was she talking about me, or did she have me mixed up with somebody else? "Thanks," I responded, "but what do you mean?"

"I mean you're always walking around dressed in a suit," she said. It was true, I wore a suit to campus on the days I worked for IBM, so I wouldn't have to go home and change.

"You've got it figured out, Shellye," my classmate said. "You've already got a job; you're walking around like a professional; people like being on your team. You've got it nailed."

It's funny how impostor syndrome rears its head—even as I was feeling more confident and competent, I still saw myself as the same old Shellye, running from classes to work, scrambling to keep everything together. I had never considered the impression I was making. I *did* have a job. I *was* taking on leadership roles on campus. Not to mention, I had job prospects and interviews already lined up. Maybe I wasn't getting all As, but I was going to graduate Wharton and get my degree, and get married, and start my career right on track with my life plan. All this time, I'd just been trying to do my best from day to day, while unbeknownst to me, I had been building a reputation for myself. People saw me, and they were forming impressions of me. I took note of that.

By the way, ever since that day, I always dress up for work. Whatever the acceptable attire for an occasion, I try to make sure I'm a notch above it. I'm not a clotheshorse, but I try to look nice. I've seen firsthand what a difference that can make in people's impressions of you. This is especially important for women in leadership. Research shows that dressing well can even improve your own mental state and self-perception.[11] And—let's be honest—I like how it feels. To this day, if I wake up overly tired or feeling unwell, I dress up. When I dress up, I tend to get compliments, and frankly, that helps me feel better.

The lesson about reputation-building has stuck with me, too. When it comes to building your reputation, the schools you attend and your performance there have an impact. I was raised to believe, and I have always believed, that a good education opens doors. But what is a "good" education? Do you have to have a degree from a prestigious university to land a great job? Do you have to earn a 4.0 to get an employer's attention? Do you have to get an advanced degree?

Initially, your education—the school you attended, your grades, and the degree you earned—will make a difference in the opportunities you will be offered right out of college. Later it won't matter as much—your reputation in the workforce will outweigh your academic record. For instance, very few people care that I have an undergraduate degree from Wharton instead of a graduate degree, because of everything I've accomplished in my career.

What can you do if you haven't had the same access to educational opportunities that other job candidates have? I have a few ideas for you.

First, no matter where you go to school, do the best work you can there, building your network and your reputation among your classmates and your professors. I'm not just talking about getting good grades; I'm talking about proving yourself in other ways, too, like publishing papers or books, serving as president of clubs and associations, or winning awards.

Second, if your undergraduate college doesn't have the prestige of, say, Harvard or MIT, you might consider entering a graduate program. Some people take out loans to finance their graduate degrees, but there are other options, like seeking out a company that will support your continued education. If you are a strong employee with potential, many companies will invest in helping you get a specialized degree, because they have a need for people with that training. The trade-off is usually that you commit to staying at the company for a certain period of time.

Finally, get creative! Whether you're earning your bachelor's degree, working toward a graduate degree, starting out at a new job, or strategizing a shift in your career, find ways to prove that you're capable, dedicated, and ambitious. Because in truth, that's what employers will be looking for at every stage of your career.

The educational system is ripe for disruption,[12] and we don't know yet how that change will manifest. Fortunately, the strategies for success will stay the same. First, seek out education, training, and job opportunities that will increase your value in the workforce. Then find ways to prove, on record, your worth and dedication. Eventually, it won't be the name of your undergraduate institution that opens doors for you; it'll be the name you make for yourself—your stellar reputation—that turns the key.

15

Be Partners in Planning

Scotty is the sort of guy who will drop everything he's doing and drive across a few states just to help his mom. He has taught me all sorts of lessons about being helpful, showing up for people you care about, and having fun. As our two-year engagement went on, my family had plenty of chances to see his kindness in action. He would even drive up to visit my family without me. He'd cook them dinner and go to one of my sisters' or brother's basketball or football games. It didn't take long for the skeptics to grow to love and admire Scotty. He did have to work hard to impress Lindy and Gran, but even they came around.

At the same time, I was getting to know his people.

"Hey, Bud, can I ask you something?" Scotty asked one day. I had gotten used to being called Bud, his catchall nickname for everyone he liked.

"Sure, what's up?"

"So my brothers are asking me, why aren't you taking my name?"

"Oh." We hadn't really talked much about that, but it had been agreed on from the start. *Is he having second thoughts?* "You know, I like my name," I said. "It's unique, and I would like to keep it. I won't ask you to take my last name." I smiled. "I just prefer to stick with Archambeau for myself. Are you changing your mind about being okay with me keeping it?"

He grinned. "No, I'm not. It is a nice name, Archambeau. I just never asked you why you wanted to keep it, so when they asked me about it, I had no answer. Well, that's what I'll tell them."

It wasn't surprising to either of us, but several of his brothers thought it was slightly emasculating that I wouldn't take his name. For his part, Scotty didn't care, didn't feel at all threatened, and truly believed that I could handle making my own decisions. Can you see what I thought was so great about this man?

Since our engagement, our late-night conversations about our philosophies and values had taken a decidedly more realist bent. Now we were engrossed in endless discussions about our future life together. Yes, Scotty became my partner in planning. We had an awful lot of decisions to make. I was about to start out on my path to becoming a CEO, but which opportunities would lead me to be the head of a company in a reasonable time frame? How soon could I become the primary breadwinner for our family? What would Scotty do with his career in the meantime? When were we going to have kids, and how did we want to raise them?

At this time, I was interviewing with companies that came to campus to recruit graduates. One such company was Xerox, and I seriously considered going to work there. It was in the technology sector, and they were offering me a good position, with management potential in the future. However, I had misgivings about whether it was the right company. I forecasted that software and computing were growth areas, but Xerox was machine-focused, and I didn't see any indications that they planned to move out of their niche. As I progressed through the interview process, my thoughts kept turning back to IBM. The company seemed like a fit with every goal I had. I'd already been working there on and off for nearly four years, and I really liked it.

So, if I was going to stay with IBM, I would need to put myself on an aggressive track immediately, first toward the management level and eventually toward the CEO role. I started plotting my strategy by researching IBM's past and current CEOs and executives. How had they risen through the ranks? Right away, I saw a pattern: Nearly all of them had started in sales. So that's what I needed to do.

Remember what I said about standing strong even when others don't agree with you? Well, when I shared my career decision with my Wharton friends, they thought I was nuts. "What do you mean? You come out of Wharton, and you're going to go into sales at IBM? That's crazy." In their minds, a Wharton grad was supposed to head to Wall Street or become a Procter & Gamble brand manager. In short, sales simply wasn't impressive enough. I suppose someone else might have caved to peer pressure or changed her plan to meet expectations. But you know what? I had a goal, I had researched the most common path to that goal, and that path was sales. So that's what I was going to do.

With my direction set, Scotty and I had more planning to do. I've always been proud of this next bit of strategy, and how well Scotty and I executed it. I was heading for graduation in June, and we were planning our wedding for August 25. If I wanted to go into sales at IBM, I would have to complete their training program, which could take twelve to eighteen months. The way IBM operated at the time, they'd hire you on a salary, and periodically you would fly to Dallas or Atlanta for a training session. I was aiming for the Large System Division, which sold mainframe computers, software, and services, because I'd have more opportunities there, so that meant my training would send me to Dallas every few weeks for the next year or more.

However, as much as I wanted to start my career with a big push, I also wanted to start a family right away. The way I figured, the sooner we had kids, the better it would be for our plans. But with both my career-building and family-building plans in play, I was likely to be pregnant (and possibly *very* pregnant) during my sales training period, so flying to Dallas was going to become a problem. But I had a solution, which I presented to Scotty one night as we were sitting on the couch in his living room.

"There's only one answer, baby," I told him, after laying out all the details. "I think we have to live in Dallas."

Scotty scratched his chin. "That could work," he said. "I just need to find a job there. I can find us a house, and you can come out after graduation and get yourself a job at the Dallas branch."

"Then I can drive to the trainings instead of flying," I said eagerly. "Maybe I can even move up some of the trainings and finish the program before the baby comes." Because for me, fast was never fast enough.

Scotty laughed and shook his head, eyes crinkling at the corners. "Archambeau, what baby? What if that baby doesn't come on your schedule? There's some things you can't plan for."

"Oh, I can try," I said, hitting him with the couch pillow.

"Well, I'm impressed," he said. "And I can't wait to start a family with you. But if we're both working and we have a young baby, we have to think about childcare. We're going to need some help."

"I thought about that, too," I said.

Scotty chuckled. "Of course you did. Lay it on me, then."

"I think we need more than just a babysitter, and I don't want to drive around to day care every day," I said. "If we hire a live-in helper, they could also help with housework, so you and I can focus on our jobs and on spending time together as a family."

"Sure, sounds great," Scotty agreed, "but that kind of help is expensive. I make decent money, but if we're buying a house, paying for a wedding, and with all the other costs of having a baby, it's going to be pretty tight. Can we really afford that?"

"I don't know, but we need to see if we can make it work," I said. "The first few years of my career are really important, and I want flexibility to concentrate on work when I have to. I don't need much else."

"If it's important to you, then let's do the numbers," Scotty said, laying a hand on my knee.

"It's important to my career, and that's important to all of us," I said.

"There you go, talking about that baby again as if it's already born." He smirked and gave my knee a gentle squeeze. "Okay, let's get the calculator."

Scotty was right, of course—some elements of this plan

weren't entirely in my control. But I wasn't going to let that stop me from setting myself up for success. Certainly, with smart planning, we could increase our odds of getting exactly what we wanted, when we wanted it. So we got to work on our budget.

We ran the numbers over and over until they worked. We made childcare our top-priority line item and arranged the rest of the budget around it. It didn't leave us much wiggle room, but we could buy a cheap house out in the Dallas suburbs with an extra room for the nanny. That location would mean a longer commute, so we would have to get two fuel-efficient cars, probably used. Scotty signed up to be a speaker on a cruise ship in exchange for a free cruise, so that saved some money on our honeymoon, and I would cover the cost of the wedding. The rest was for our savings and incidentals.

There it was: our plan. Right away, Scotty started applying for promotion opportunities in Dallas, and within a couple of months he landed a job as a product manager. We flew out to Dallas on a weekend to shop for a house. Then Scotty was gone, off to Dallas, while I was finishing school and planning our wedding.

I wanted a big wedding, and since I was paying for it, that's what I got. First of all, everyone who was close to me, I wanted them standing next to me. Our families all came, and our guest list included everybody from my past—Los Angeles to Connecticut to New Jersey to Philadelphia—and Scotty's college buddies. We ended up inviting almost four hundred people, and over three hundred actually showed up. Scotty had a connection to Alfie Pollitt, a legendary Philly bandleader who had toured with Teddy Pendergrass, and with Alfie's help we threw a big party with hours of dancing.

The one thing we forgot: to explain our unique names to Alfie before he announced us on the dance floor. Scotty's real name is Clarence Scott, and I would remain Shellye Archambeau. As we made our big entrance, in front of hundreds of our family and friends, Alfie grabbed the microphone and announced:

"Introducing... Mr. and Mrs. Scotty Scott!"

Scotty was laughing so hard he was crying as he pulled me in for a kiss.

Other than that, it all went off without a hitch. After the wedding, Scotty and I jetted off to a nice hotel in New York, and the next morning we got on separate planes, each of us with business to take care of. We didn't see each other again for a week, when we finally met up for our honeymoon, a Caribbean cruise. Then we moved into our suburban Dallas ranch house and got to work.

That's how my real adventure began: the adventure of adulthood. I sure hoped I was ready.

PART THREE

LIVING THE PLAN

16

Execute the Plan

Once upon a time, there was a woman who got everything she wanted: a loving husband, a promising career, and a baby on the way. And then, reality set in.

My grand plan executed perfectly. I got pregnant right away, and thanks to our Dallas move, I was accelerating my sales training program at IBM. After the baby was born, I planned to take five weeks of maternity leave and then return to work in time for a big conference, hitting the ground running as a salesperson on quota.

Well, I accelerated a bit too fast. I finished the sales training early and ended up going on quota while eight months pregnant. Oh well, they say life happens while you're making plans.

In between long workdays, the commute, trying to furnish a home within our budget, and preparing a nursery, Scotty and I started going to birthing classes, where I half-heartedly practiced breathing exercises. I'd be lying down on the floor, propped up by pillows, with Scotty beside me, holding my hand and counting out the tempo: "Long breath in…short breath, short breath, short breath…long breath in…" After one or two rounds of this, I'd start whispering a list of groceries we needed to pick up or trying to discuss our schedule. Because really, I knew I wanted an epidural.

What can I say? I'm not into pain, and I was glad to be able to opt out of that part of childbirth. All respect to the women who choose natural childbirth—that just wasn't me. I don't handle pain well. Strike that, I don't handle it at all. I am such a wimp that I've been known to scream after getting a paper cut. I wanted to skip the terror and move right into celebrating the miracle of life. Scotty supported my choice—actually, since we're being honest, he didn't want to see me in pain, and he hates the sight of blood, so he was fine to just join me after it was all over. He wasn't planning to be in the delivery room at all. As a result, I saw birthing classes as a waste of precious time. I went through the motions, but mentally, Scotty and I were both completely writing it off. I was getting an epidural, end of story.

They say you get the child you need, not exactly the one you planned for. Kethlyn let us know right off the bat how she felt about us making all the decisions for her.

I woke early in the morning on June 17. (Who sleeps in those last weeks of pregnancy, anyway?) As usual, I had to go to the bathroom right away. I eased out of our bed, trying not to disturb Scotty, supporting my belly as I rolled off the mattress onto my feet. The sun was just coming up, and I could see the outline of our quiet street out the window. I waddled into the bathroom and sat. I felt pressure, but when I tried, nothing happened. And then it hit me: a wave of cramping.

Is this it?! I thought. *Am I in labor?!* But something was funny. I felt more cramping just a few beats later. Wasn't I supposed to get a longer break between contractions?

"Scotty?" I called out. I could hear him rustling around in bed. As I stood up and walked to the bathroom door, another cramp hit me.

"Scotty?" I said again. "Babe, I think I'm having contractions."

He sat straight up in bed. "Oh wow, okay. I'll get the stopwatch."

As he went to get it, I felt another wave, stronger this time, and I bent over. *This is too fast. Aren't they supposed to start slow?* I wondered. *Well, don't get anxious, just breathe.*

The stopwatch confirmed my suspicions. The contractions were less than five minutes apart. *I can't believe this is happening. I hope I'm ready.* Scotty got on the phone with the doctor, and I started getting dressed, pausing now and then, breathing heavily as the contractions rolled through. Then Scotty's warm arm was around my shoulders. "Bud, there's no need to panic, but we have to get you to the hospital right away."

Luckily, the hospital was only a fifteen-minute drive, because by the time we got there, I was in full-blown labor. Eight centimeters dilated. The baby was coming—no time for the epidural. Me, the person who can't handle even the tiniest pain—I was about to go in for a natural birth.

Picture this: I'm in the triage area on a gurney, the awful fluorescent lights blazing down. The nurses are trying to put an IV in my arm. At this point, I'm screaming in pain, begging for drugs each time I catch my breath. Scotty is holding my hand

and stroking my face, trying to calm me down. The nurses are yelling to each other, trying to locate a doctor. It's chaos. Finally, we are whisked away by people in scrubs, and in the excitement, they just assume that Scotty wants to be in the room for the birth. So they put a gown on him, and in we all go to the delivery room. Exactly *not* how we planned it.

I had done absolutely none of the mental exercises to prepare for pain, and now I am completely off the deep end. Poor Scotty is so panicked, all he can do is squeeze my hand as I scream. When the pain of birth breaks for a second, I yell, "Scotty! Give me back my hand!" He had been squeezing so hard it was bruised afterward.

I'll give Kethlyn this: She's a decisive person, and thankfully she knew it was time to be born. As ridiculous as the whole scene was, it all ended in fifteen minutes, like this:

I'm pushing for all I'm worth, when I hear someone exclaim, "Here it comes..." I feel the physical relief just as the pronouncement is made—"It's a girl!" Then I hear my baby cry. The nurse carries her to my bedside. Briefly I see a pale little thing, her eyes closed, her little fists moving fitfully, before the nurse takes her away to clean her up. I close my eyes, my chest rising and falling heavily as I catch my breath. I'm sore, exhausted, relieved, and so, so happy. Scotty leans over the bed, and before he can say anything, I say, "You survived!" He laughs and kisses me.

From that moment, we were forever a family. It didn't matter anymore what our plans had been. At this point, I didn't care about anything but our daughter.

When I was wheeled into my semi-private room afterward, I was soaked with sweat and hoarse from screaming. From a fifteen-minute birth. The woman sharing my room sat up and looked at me.

"Are you the one who just delivered?" she asked. "Was that you I heard screaming?"

Cringing a little, I nodded. Apparently, I had let the whole hospital know that Kethlyn was on her way.

⌒

For the next few weeks, Kethlyn and I were totally at each other's mercy—that unique phase of parenthood where your entire identity is dismantled and rebuilt in the light of your child's face, in the dark of the exhausted nights, in the weakness of vulnerability, and in the strength of life's miracles. She was so beautiful, she took my breath away.

She also stripped down any beliefs I'd had about being somehow stronger or more capable than others, about being able to handle having a newborn and going back to work within weeks. What happened to Shellye the master strategist? The Shellye who was so sure she had it all under control—where did she go? Suddenly a big part of me felt like I had no idea what I was doing, none whatsoever. Once again, I was just one person in the great big world—just Shellye, alone and anxious. I had not felt this vulnerable in a long time.

Throughout my life, I have always leaned on family when I am vulnerable, and they have strengthened me. In those early weeks of parenthood—and anytime, really—Scotty would have carried my full weight if I needed it. Now and then, I suppose I did. His calmness and his ability to take anything in stride— that centered me. Mom was there for me, too, flying out to help us for two entire weeks. Soon, we had additional help in the form of Becky, the nanny who arrived shortly after Kethlyn did, and we fell into a routine. We'd had a great nurse in the hospital who suggested that, even though I was breastfeeding, we should use a bottle for Kethlyn's two a.m. feeding, so Scotty could take care of that one. (I definitely married the right man!) As an added bonus, this would ultimately make for an easier transition to the bottle when I went back to work.

Long before I returned to work, we determined a schedule. Scotty would take the two a.m. feeding. I would do the six a.m. feeding, and Becky would take responsibility for Kethlyn at eight. Scotty would go to work very early—five or six o'clock. I would leave around eight. Becky would have Kethlyn for the day, and Scotty would arrive home around four thirty to take over. I'd get home by seven. As we settled into this routine, eventually my sleep schedule would go back to normal, and my anxiety would stabilize, too. But I didn't know that yet.

Still, knowing we had a schedule in place was helpful. When I found myself worrying about returning to work, I'd remind myself: *I planned for this. It's going to be okay.* It wasn't easy, though. If I had known how hard it would be to go back after five weeks, I don't think I would have put it in the plan. But it was my dedication to—my trust in—the plan that kept me moving forward. I knew Scotty and I had strategized in accordance with my ambition, and when I thought about it that way, I wanted to get back on track.

Ugh! I still shake my head when I think about twenty-three-year-old Shellye and how much *hustle* she had. For example, my first week back at work would coincide with my first big sales conference. With that event right up ahead of me, I started working out as soon as I possibly could after Kethlyn was born. After all, the conference wasn't just a conference, it was also a retreat, and I would need to be in a bathing suit. Who does that?

Even just packing for the conference felt like a big deal: trying on my clothes to see if any of them would fit, stopping now and then to soothe my crying daughter or pump some milk while Scotty and Becky were hammering out a schedule for taking care of Kethlyn in my absence. Scotty was worried about me, I think, but he never gave me a moment of grief about running off to a conference so soon. He understood the importance of this opportunity, and he supported me, fully. Thank goodness, because even the thought of leaving was causing a grief I could hardly put words to. The sort that wells up from someplace deeper than your heart, someplace biological, genetic.

I did it, though. I got the suitcase packed, kissed my husband and child goodbye a hundred times, and got into a cab, headed for the airport. As it was pulling away, I looked out the window. I could see the reflection of my face, just its outline superimposed on the streets and cars of Dallas. *Wow*, I thought. *I am really doing this. I'm going back to my life at IBM.* But I felt so different now. I *was* different. Stepping forward into the career I had planned—that part felt exciting. But the overwhelming sadness? That I hadn't anticipated. What a potent mix of emotions.

In the airport, I couldn't stop thinking about Kethlyn, and then, as if to accentuate the point, my milk started to leak. I had to run to the bathroom and change my breast pads. That's when the old doubting voice crept in. *Can I do this?* I honestly didn't know. But I was going to find out.

At that moment, if you had told me the conference was

canceled, I would have been back home in five minutes, holding my baby. But if you'd told me I should skip the conference, that being with my baby was more important than this major foundational step in my career—I don't know. Actually, I suppose I do know. The company wasn't forcing me to come back to work so soon. This was my choice. I went to the conference because I knew Kethlyn would be all right with my husband and nanny, and because I knew the conference was an opportunity that, if missed, could set me back considerably. I made a rational choice, and I paid an emotional and physical price. Leaving Kethlyn was so hard, my heart ached and so did my breasts. I stopped nursing cold turkey so I could nurse her as much as possible before I went back to work. The pain and discomfort from this decision were very real. But I'd do it again.

Remember what this moment meant for me: I had been planning for this since high school. I'd gone to school for it. I had strategized for it. I'd completed my training—at an accelerated pace—for it. This would be my first real moment of grown-up Shellye, at work, doing the job I had been hired for. Yes, I had been on quota for a few weeks before Kethlyn's birth, but it wasn't the same—I wasn't a normal sales rep in those weeks; I was the new, super pregnant girl. Finally, at this conference, I could be seen for my abilities and accomplishments. I was ready to be Shellye the sales rep—nothing more or less.

More importantly, the three-day conference came only once a year, and it was crucial to making my quota. Here I would meet the decision makers for all my clients: 7-Eleven, Neiman Marcus, grocery store chains, major national retailers. It was time to make an impression and begin developing relationships. I needed them to see my face, to know me, because you bet I was going to sell to them later. I had to be there, I wanted to be there, and once I crossed the threshold, I was truly and deeply happy to be there. More or less, this was the theme of my first few years as a wife, mother, and working professional: constantly making choices. Scratch that. It's been the theme of my entire adult life: not sacrifices—choices.

In the end, that conference went well, if quickly. Honestly, I hardly remember a moment of it now, but I do remember coming home. Tired and happy, I stepped out of the cab and walked up to my front door. The house was dark and quiet. Kethlyn must have gone down already. I opened the door to find Scotty stretched out on a chair in the family room. He got up sleepily. *He looks more exhausted than I feel*, I thought. I gave him a big hug. Then, quietly and as fast as I could, I rushed in to see my baby.

She was just like an angel, her light cocoa skin all plump, with the hint of a double chin. She had the tiniest ears and hardly any hair, just thin brown wisps. As she slept, her lips moved a little—like she was talking in her sleep. I was overwhelmed with love. And my milk started leaking.

～

A few days after the conference, Scotty and I got a call from our friend Jerry.

"Hey, what are you two up to tonight? We just heard there's a great band coming to the club. Want to go?"

I almost broke out laughing hysterically, but I managed to keep it to a chuckle. "Jerry, are you crazy? Remember, we have a baby now?"

"Oh yeah," he said. "I forgot. But you can get a sitter, right?"

Now I did laugh out loud. "Um, no, I can't get a sitter for tonight without notice. You go have fun without us."

After I hung up, I caught Scotty looking at me with a funny smile.

"What?" I asked, still laughing a little.

"Archambeau, it looks like we're going to be doing all our dancing at home these days."

He held out his hand, and we slowly swayed around the family room, in silence. I can't speak for what Scotty was thinking, but my thoughts were clear: *This is real. Our old life is gone forever . . . and that's okay.*

It turned out we wouldn't have enough time to dance, even in the family room. For the next two years, all we did was work, cook, eat, and sleep. Days blurred together; nights were too short. Of course, we shared countless moments of joy, but they were surrounded by endless responsibilities, and never enough sleep. Motherhood is hard! Especially early motherhood. So many demands, not enough hours—it's no wonder many women become overly stressed and self-critical during this period of our lives. At least you can find a little comfort in knowing that it's difficult for everyone; you aren't alone.

I struggled most with trying to help Kethlyn when she was crying. It was so frustrating that she couldn't tell me what was wrong. "Just talk to me!" I'd plead with her—but of course she couldn't, and we both wound up deeper in anguish. Scotty seemed to handle it better, to take her crying in stride. Or maybe that was only my perception. I just didn't want my baby to suffer, and it tortured me when I didn't know how to help her.

Kethlyn, however, was developing well. She was beautiful,

and so smart, and we marveled at how quickly she was learning. With Becky's help, our baby girl was thriving, and despite the busyness and blur, I knew life was working out exactly as we had planned it. We had strategized and budgeted and made trade-offs so we could keep working, knowing our daughter was safe and happy. I learned to put my trust in my decisions, and as the weeks went by, I grew more confident. It was all working out just fine.

What's more, I was seeing the power of our strategic planning. If we had changed even one element of our financial plan—if we hadn't prioritized childcare in our budget, if we'd moved into a more expensive home, if we'd leased new cars or spent more on entertainment—*this* wouldn't have been possible. The feeling of security I now had, knowing my daughter was well cared for—I had traded other things for it, and I'd made a good trade. I said a little thank-you to the Shellye and Scotty of the past, and I poured myself into my work with greater confidence.

17

Understand the Field

At IBM, I was just beginning to understand how things really worked. No longer the shiny new employee, after a year or two I started to see some patterns. Specifically, I saw patterns among the executives. If I was going to become the CEO of IBM, I needed to get onto the executive track; but at times, it felt like the executives existed on some other planet, and I was watching from millions of miles away. Invisible.

So, what did it take to become visible like them? IBM had a lot of big meetings where I watched how the executives carried themselves and behaved. They always seemed prepared to take the podium, and most impressively, every last one of them was an excellent speaker. They looked comfortable in front of a crowd, so at home in their skin. I most definitely did not have those skills. Yes, I had done some presentations at Wharton, made a few speeches for various organizations—but stepping up in front of hundreds of people and making impromptu remarks? That was so outside my comfort zone that my pulse rose just thinking about it. Clearly, I had to work on that, and I had an idea how.

One evening, I came home with a brochure for Toastmasters. I waited until Kethlyn was in her crib and Scotty had finished his dinner. As he pushed back from the table with a sigh, I got up and placed the pamphlet next to him, clearing his plate with my other hand.

"Babe, I want to talk to you about Toastmasters. I think it's something I need to try."

He picked up the glossy pamphlet and unfolded it. "Toastmasters, that's a speaking club, right? A couple of guys I know have done it."

"Right. It's for learning to be a better public speaker. They have you practice talking to groups on different topics, and they give you direct feedback until you get to be good at it." I put the dishes in the sink and started running water over them. "I think I need to get good at it if I want to be an executive."

Scotty stood from the table, walked over, and leaned against the kitchen counter to look me in the face. "Sure. You know I support you, Shellye, but can you take on any more responsibilities right now?"

I smiled, knowing exactly how tired I looked—because he looked the same way. "Well, that's what I wanted to ask you about. It's two nights a week, after work."

Scotty's face shifted. I could see him processing what that meant: two nights a week taking care of things at home, feeding Kethlyn and putting her down, without my help. Two nights a week we might not see each other for more than a moment.

I turned off the water and opened the dishwasher, letting him think as I loaded the dishes into it. Then I turned back to him and put a hand on my hip. "I know this is a lot to ask of you—"

"Yeah, it's an ask all right," he said, but his eyes were smiling. "But if you've thought about this and it's something you need, I'm not about to stand in your way. Tell me how you think we're going to make this work."

Over the next few days, we made a plan for those precious few hours a week. There simply wasn't any money to spare, so time was our only resource. We carved out that time like it was gold—which it was. We streamlined our already efficient plans so Scotty could be a one-man show, and off I went to Toastmasters.

In reality, we both knew what this choice represented: We were prioritizing my career over his, just as we discussed before we got married. Scotty wasn't investing time in his own career development, because he was investing in *mine*. I knew how much it meant that my husband and daughter were at home while I spent time and energy on my career. I am still grateful, and I always knew I would do my best to repay them by providing the best life I could for them.

As I moved steadily in that direction, time passed quickly. You know how you look around and everything seems finally to have become stable and predictable—which is how you know it's time to shake things up? By 1986, Kethlyn was bopping around on her own, chattering and laughing. I had completed Toastmasters, and if I'm honest, it improved my confidence so much that I even had better posture. I was doing great sales numbers, and I was feeling ready to take my next step.

While doing my best at the job I had, I had continued watching and learning, understanding the field that lay in front of me and how best to play it so I would end up in the CEO's seat. Since that eye-opening meeting with my high school counselor, I'd been on a journey of investigation and advancement. First question: How do you become a CEO? I looked around at CEOs, where they came from, and how they got there. One thing for sure: I didn't find any who looked like me, so I knew I would need to work hard to improve my odds. How did I improve my odds? By going to Wharton, working hard in my classes and at my part-time job, getting involved in clubs, and developing my reputation. Done. Next question: Where do I want to do this? I predicted I'd find growing opportunities in technology, particularly software and computing, so off I went, securing my spot at a top company, IBM. (I mean, if I'm going to set out to be a CEO, why not aim for the top company, right?) So far, my strategic choice, starting off in sales at IBM, was paying off. But what came next? I knew I needed to advance toward an executive position, and along the way I needed general management experience. The first real place to get that would be a branch manager role. On and on I went, jumping across milestones, making each choice in service of my goal.

Of course, I was doing all of this on a timeline, because if you don't have timelines, then it's really easy to become complacent, to let things linger, to let life take over. If you have timelines, and you stick to them unwaveringly, then you get things done. So I looked around at the current branch managers at IBM, and I noticed most had gotten their jobs in their thirties. Okay. So I set my timeline: I want to be a branch manager when I'm thirty.

Meanwhile, I was approaching another next step in our family plan. Before getting married, Scotty and I had discussed how many children we wanted. We had agreed on having two, if we had a boy and a girl. If they were the same sex, we would try one more time. Three max. Well, after Kethlyn's chaotic, no-epidural delivery, I hadn't so much as mentioned that second child. Scotty had given me space, but with Kethlyn now two years old, he started raising the topic—more and more frequently. Finally, I was looking at our little roly-poly angel and hearing those funny thoughts about "another one." *Another little cherub...Just don't think about the actual birth. Think about the miracles! The miracles are what matter.*

Soon I had talked myself into it, and in mid-1987, it was official. I was pregnant again, filled with those now-familiar feelings of excitement and nausea, fear and hormones, physical discomfort and vivid dreams. Someone new was on the way to join our family.

18

No Second Thoughts

One evening in the early fall, just after dinner, I was rocking Kethlyn on my lap. "Doll baby," I cooed as she started to doze. "What do you think your new brother or sister will look like? What should we name him or her?" I stroked her hair, lost in the moment, as Scotty sat down next to us on the couch.

"Ahem," he said quietly. "I got some news today."

I turned to face him. "Uh-oh," I whispered with a smile. "What kind of news?"

Scotty raised his beer. "I got a promotion. If I want it. There's a customer center in Harrisburg, Pennsylvania, that needs a manager."

"Wow," I said. "Congratulations, that's great. Let me put her down and then we can talk about it."

As I tucked Kethlyn into her crib, I thought about what this could mean. I didn't have to think about whether this was a good move for Scotty. It was, and it fit with our plans to follow our careers where they took us. *Moving back east would bring us closer to our families. I could move upward, make it into a promotion. But I'm pregnant. Would they give me a good job if they knew?*

I walked back into the kitchen, plopped back down on the couch, and said, "Okay, let's do it. But I'm not telling anybody I'm pregnant."

Scotty tilted his head. "Okay, but why not?"

"Well, I think I can go for a senior job if there is one. But there's a risk that they won't hire a pregnant woman to a senior sales job. Not if there's a man who can do the job without going on maternity leave."

He took my hand. "I guess I can see that. Well, then, we better do this before anybody finds out."

"I do want to tell my mom and dad, though. They'll be so happy we're coming home, and with a new grandbaby on the way." I smiled, thinking about how nice it would be to drive a few hours instead of flying to them.

"Now, Shellye, there's something else I wanted to talk to you about," Scotty said. "I've been thinking, if we're doing this, it should be the last move we make for my career."

My smile deepened. I knew what he meant. This was the last move for his career, because from now on, we'd be going where *my* career took us. With a second baby on the way, it would soon be time for Scotty to follow through on our plan and become a stay-at-home dad.

⌒

If you have never worked for a big corporation, let me confirm the rumors: They can be cutthroat environments, with so many people trying to climb over each other and up the ladder. On the other hand, working for a big company, you constantly have options and opportunities. There's a lot to be said for finding your path through the halls of a corporation; it certainly was working for me.

I was doing well at IBM, so it never really occurred to me that there'd be any trouble moving to Harrisburg with a better job. I simply asked my branch manager to make a few calls. He spoke with the local branch manager, who identified a senior sales opportunity. I interviewed—didn't tell anybody I was pregnant—and landed it. Done.

Something else was working in our favor, too. Neither Scotty nor I harbored second thoughts about this move. We knew this was the right decision for us, because we had discussed all our life plans long before even getting married. This was a clear step on the trajectory we had in mind. Just like my parents before us, we never worried over the disruption or freaked out about the details of the move. We took it in stride, confident we were heading in the right direction.

Those secure foundations mean the world when you're a young mother working full-time with a new baby on the way. I can't imagine what it would have been like if I had been questioning whether I was making the right choice or agonizing over how to find a job in a new city. It was challenging enough to learn my new job (yes, I had taken a leap up and landed at the bottom of my next learning curve), to find our way around Harrisburg, to make plans for the new baby, and of course to settle into a new home. I didn't have time for doubts. I was too busy moving forward with my plan.

19

Delegate

Before Kheaton was due, when we had just moved into our new house, my mother came to visit for a few days. When I say our house was new, it wasn't just new to us; it had just been built. So there was no landscaping to speak of, and I really wanted flowers. I had a vision of shade and blossoms for our perfect little home. Since we didn't have any money, I started doing the landscaping myself. My weekends were mostly spent digging in the dirt, carting mulch around, and planting. It gave me a lot of pride to see a tree in the yard that I had planted myself.

But everywhere I turned, there was something else to take care of. While the landscaping was coming along, there was still decorating to do in the house, and so many other things that had to happen before I felt our life would qualify as "settled." So I called Mom, and I asked if she could come down and help me make some curtains and other finishings. We spent our evenings cutting and sewing and chatting, with Mom sharing her advice on life and marriage. Yes, she always had an opinion, but she was usually right.

One evening, after the sun had set, Mom and I were in the dining room we had converted into a temporary sewing room. On one end of the table sat the sewing machine, cords hanging down for the foot pedal and the power connection. Mom was hunched in front of it, under the glare of a tall desk lamp, her hands guiding fabric under the needle as the machine hummed. The other end of the table was covered with a makeshift cutting board, fabric pieces stacked into units, patterns, pins, scissors, measuring tape, and other sewing tools. Against the wall, we'd set up an ironing board, where I stood, pinning the seams of what appeared to be endless fabric panels, in preparation for stitching.

"Shellye, just remember," Mom said to me, taking her foot off the sewing machine pedal as she finished the seam, "there are lots of things I do not know how to do."

I stopped pinning. "What do you mean?"

"You know." She shrugged. "I do not know *how* to wash windows. I do not know *how* to put out the trash. I don't know *how* to change the oil in the car. I don't know *how*..."

A smile dawned on my face. "Ohh, I get it," I said. "Those are the things Daddy does."

Her lips curled up and her eyes smiled. "Yes, they are," she said, "and I will never learn how to do those things. Shellye, once you demonstrate that you know how to do something, it will become your job. You need to leave some things alone and let somebody else carry some of the responsibilities."

That may be some of the best advice I've ever received—

and, as a woman and a Type A personality, some of the hardest advice to follow. It doesn't just apply to housework, mind you, but to everything assumed to be part of a woman's purview. In those early days of my marriage, I took on responsibility for everything I could see or touch, from dinner to landscaping to decorating to our social plans.

It's a well-documented fact that, decades after most women entered the workplace, we're still doing the majority of the housework.[13] What my mother was trying to tell me was *why* and *how* that comes to be. It isn't quite as simple as the tempting generalization of "men don't see or care when things need to be done." As a matter of fact, Scotty was a great help with everything, always ready to contribute. But that's the thing—in my mind, Scotty was *helping*, but the responsibility was always mine.

I believe this pattern is passed down through habits, almost unconsciously, from generation to generation. It began simply— "Scotty, can you help me with the laundry?"—and it continued when, as he combined different clothing items into one load, I silently (or not so silently) assessed his ability to do the task. I was managing him in these little chores, never fully releasing the responsibility for the job.

Why couldn't I accept my husband doing the laundry his way? Why did I feel the ultimate responsibility fell to me? I'm not sure exactly, but at least I wasn't alone in that tendency. Conventional wisdom reasons it this way: Because domestic work is historically seen as "women's work," women are expecting to be judged on the quality of the domestic work, whether they actually did the work or not.[14] In other words, if my husband steps out in a wrinkled shirt, I'm the one who worries about what people think—of me, not him.

This is old-fashioned thinking, and it's neither logical nor practical. With every passing generation, the imprints of these gender roles are fading. Yet the habits remain, and these habits have their impact not just at home but in the workplace as well.

Here's how this comes into play at work: There's a school of thought—something you hear a lot in professional development circles—that each of us should figure out what our strengths and weaknesses are, and then we should strengthen the weaknesses. To me, this makes no sense at all. I say you ought to strengthen your strengths, because that's how you become most valuable to your team. Yet I know many successful professional women who still believe that they have to know how to do everything and do it well. For example, a respected CEO apologizes because she doesn't cook. I don't know one man who feels deficient based on his cooking skills. A woman might berate herself for lacking a seemingly basic skill, like knowing how to format a document, while a man will readily hand such a task over to a member of admin staff, because that's what admins do. In short, at home and at work, women tend to believe we are cheating if we accept help, or we are inadequate if we can't seamlessly transition between a wide variety of tasks.

This mentality is stifling at home, and at work it can slow the progress of your career. In order to rise in an organization, you have to be able to take your responsibilities, to delegate tasks to the right team members, and to seek guidance from others as you face new challenges. It seems evident, on the surface, that we shouldn't expect ourselves to be perfect polymaths; but I've known many women who have gotten stuck in their careers because they were unable to master a skill they could have delegated, unwilling to delegate a task someone else could do, or unwilling to seek guidance when they needed it.

I like to say, "The more you do, the less you get paid." Your ability to get work done through others is exactly why you get promoted up the career ladder. I don't mean that senior people don't work hard. Most do. But they take on less creation personally. They inspire, direct, review, edit, and enable their teams to get the necessary work done to execute on their strategy.

At home, my mother, in her own way, was telling me to set my priorities, choose my own tasks, and delegate the rest to other people. It would take me a long time to put her advice into regular practice, but at least I could start. When I realized I truly couldn't handle the gardening, and Scotty didn't have the time or desire to do it, either, we hired a landscape company. Of course, we had Becky to help with Kethlyn. What else could I let go? That question was about to become deeply important to me.

20

Embrace Your Limits

After Kethlyn's dramatic surprise appearance, and with my due date approaching, my doctor told me he was worried I'd drop the next baby while walking down the street. I was bigger with this pregnancy, because the baby was bigger, so we agreed to schedule a delivery fully three weeks before my due date. I was all good with this plan. I was uncomfortable and ready to be finished. Plus, this way I could be sure I'd have more control over the experience, and I'd get my epidural. In other words, I was not going through that pain again. Period.

Well, thank goodness we made that plan, because even three weeks early, my darling son was eight pounds and seven ounces. No wonder I'd been uncomfortable—I could have had a ten-pound baby if he'd gone full term! I was glad to have him in my arms instead, my wrinkled little boy, with his skin still dusty from the journey. He never seemed to mind being born early.

He quickly grew into a luminous, sweet, and charming infant. We named him Kheaton. It was 1988, and our family was complete.

And by the way, that swing coat I bought in college? I wore it during both my pregnancies.

Kheaton was immediately everyone's baby—including his three-year-old sister's. She loved him fiercely and protectively, his guardian against the world. Once again, those first few weeks were like another life—me and my babies, in our own little world. I would sit on the couch with Kheaton nestled on his back along my closed legs. I'd rock him side to side by shifting my knees, holding his tiny, fat feet in my hands, leaning over to kiss them. Kethlyn would peer at him, touching him and naming his parts—"head," "nose," "mouth"—as I reminded her to be gentle. In the evenings, Scotty would come home, and we'd be all smiles, taking a million pictures—exhausted, yes, but surrounded in love.

But it was the 1980s, and I only felt comfortable taking six weeks of maternity leave. All too quickly, it was time to return to work. And not just work, but *commitments* as well. There is no PC way to say this, so I'll just be frank: Scotty and I, as IBM's only African American couple in management in Harrisburg, often served as a token couple at high-profile events. IBM would buy out a table at an event, and we would have seats. As a result, our work-related social calendar was quite a bit busier than that of the average professional couple. Scotty and I both love to meet people, so on one level it was thrilling to have so many opportunities to make new connections, and...it was also just another level of responsibility. Our workdays now extended into the evenings.

This continued for the first few years of Kheaton's life. We made a point to spend all the quality time we could with our beautiful children, but we definitely relied on our nanny more than ever before. Becky, our nanny in Dallas, had come along with us for the first year in Harrisburg, but then we had to find someone new. Ultimately we settled on a male au pair named Torben, a conscious choice to show our children that men and women are equally competent caretakers. Around this time, Kethlyn was old enough to start getting involved in activities, so we had even more added to the calendar: ballet, tap, karate lessons, and Jack and Jill, a group for African American mothers and children. Then I was asked to join the board of a nonprofit organization that centered around people with disabilities, and I eagerly accepted, despite my full schedule, because nonprofit board experience is a terrific development and networking opportunity.

At this point, I had not a single spare minute in a day, ever. The stress began to wear on me. I'd catch myself wondering, *Is this really what I signed up for? Is this how it's going to be forever?* Of course, it wasn't always going to be so stressful. Right? Often I would remind myself, *Shellye, you're very fortunate to have a wonderful family, and a good job, and plenty of options. This is the life you've chosen. Enjoy it.* But as much as I wanted to, enjoying these things wasn't always easy. In fact, around this time, finding joy started to feel truly, deeply difficult. I don't know how to describe it exactly, other than to say I started to feel moody, as if something deep inside me was using up all my energy. I was just so tired all the time. I didn't want to get out of bed if I could avoid it. But I could never avoid it, and as I forced myself to get up and follow through on all my responsibilities, the cavern inside me grew deeper and darker. I was losing myself.

I refused to let anyone see how I was feeling. Not my friends, not my kids, not Scotty. *This is ridiculous*, I would say to myself. *I have a great husband and amazing kids. My career is moving the way I expect it to. I've got all these great activities and interesting people in my life. What's my problem? I don't have the right to feel bad. Everything is going my way.* But for all my frustrated self-talk, I couldn't negotiate myself out of my depression. And so, finally, I gave in and made an appointment to see a psychologist. I was twenty-eight years old.

Those therapy sessions were a big eye-opener for me. I had never stopped to consider my overwhelming drive to "be good"—to be *seen* as a good person—and what that was doing to my actual self-worth. In all my actions, I was giving as much of myself away as I could. If anyone needed anything, or even just wanted anything I could provide, I would give it. I'd been this way since childhood: I just wanted to be liked. What I needed to learn was that I *was* liked, and that even well-liked people say no sometimes.

For all my drive and ambition, I had never developed an ambition to be loving and patient with myself. Even writing those words—they sound a little silly to me still, after all these years. In those days, self-love and patience were out of the question. But I needed to learn that taking care of *me* was just as important as every other priority. I started by regularly carving out time to exercise. Something about pushing my body to physical, sweaty fatigue—it helped me not just stay in shape but also clear my mind and better manage stress.

In addition to encouraging me to prioritize self-care, the therapist helped me understand the unrealistic bar I was setting for myself—and that I was the only person expecting such high achievement. Nobody else needed me to be perfect. I let this new idea sink in, and I started to let myself off the hook: To forgive myself when I was too tired to work out. To allow myself to stay in bed fifteen minutes longer. To have a little fun, and not just the appearance of fun.

Next, I had to start learning to say no. For me, this was not a simple process. I am a person who truly wants to be helpful, whenever possible. To this day, I still try to help everyone who needs it. So I had to find a way to be helpful without giving time or energy I could not afford to give. I began by evaluating requests differently: not in terms of whether I could help in *theory*, but whether I could *realistically* be useful. I had to tell people, "I don't have the time." I learned to be clear about this, instead of hedging and putting people off. I still do this, by the way. I always try to tell people clearly when I can't get involved. But there's a follow-through, which is, if I can, I try to offer another option. Usually I give people a referral to someone who can help; sometimes I recommend an alternate solution. That way, the person who needs help isn't left hanging. They know where to go. And I've managed to preserve my time.

Finally, I had to learn to ask myself about what was really important. I'm talking about a daily question: "What's really important for me today?" The answer to that question could be different from day to day, but I had to have an answer. I had to focus on what *I wanted*, not what I thought the world wanted from me. And that made the difference. As I found my limits, I internalized the concept that I can have anything I want, just not all at the same time.

Mom had tried to tell me. Several times. She tried to remind me to put myself first, to set boundaries, to be reasonable about my expectations. Given that she's a woman who accomplishes daily more than most other people do in a week, I ought to have listened to her. But I think this may be one of the lessons that is often learned the hard way. You have to find your own limits.

Because you're reading this, I imagine you're an ambitious person who is working hard to achieve your aspirations. I suspect at some point you too will find yourself at a place where you will need to reassess your life, to settle into reality, and to find a way to make things work that doesn't involve stressing yourself into a depression. It concerns me to see how many people believe they must accomplish everything on their own, without compromising anything but their own well-being. If you "have it all" but sacrifice yourself, what do you really have in the end?

It really is like they say on planes: Put your own oxygen mask on first, then help other people.

21

Live Your Values

It was Saturday morning, early. I woke slowly, lazily, warm in bed. I could smell something cooking. *Mmm, breakfast.* I smiled and snuggled back into the covers. Next to me, Scotty stirred in his sleep.

Wait. If Scotty is in bed, who is in the kitchen?

I jumped out of bed in a flash. "Scotty! The kids are in the kitchen!"

As I snatched on my robe and barreled down the hallway toward the stairs, I could hear him behind me. "Kethlyn! Kheaton! What are you doing?" I called. Just as I reached the top of the stairs, a very firm, very small voice came from the kitchen below.

"Don't come down here!"

I skidded to a halt, putting an arm out to stop my husband, who was a step behind.

"What's that, Doll?"

"Don't come down here," Kethlyn said again. I couldn't see her from the landing. I heard dishes clanking in the kitchen.

I turned to Scotty. He shrugged.

"Okay..." I said slowly. "Are you sure you don't need help or anything?"

"No," she said. "Just stay up there."

Kethlyn was almost six years old, and her little brother was three. We had a gas cooktop, which they were clearly using, unsupervised. But I couldn't smell anything burning.

"What do we do?" I asked Scotty.

He looked as confused as I felt. "Well," he said, scratching his cheek, "I guess we stay here. We're close enough to help if there's a fire." A slow smile spread across his face. "Sounds to me like we don't have another choice."

I let my breath out in a long sigh, shaking my head. "I guess not," I said, wrapping my robe around me. "So, we wait then."

We sat down on the landing.

You won't be surprised to learn that Scotty and I had discussed our parenting goals before we were even married. We settled on a unified philosophy: We wanted our kids to be self-sufficient, confident, and caring. Every parenting choice we ever made, we held it up to that rubric. And now we were having our first real test.

It was exciting and a little silly, sitting at the top of the steps in my robe with my husband, waiting to find out what our children were doing downstairs. We could hear them chattering, plates scraping. We chuckled nervously and squeezed each other's hands, and I tried to stay calm and push images of cuts and injuries out of my head.

After what felt like hours, two little figures stepped into view at the bottom of the stairs. My heart fluttered. They were dressed in their best, Kethlyn in her Sunday dress, Kheaton wearing nice pants and a little vest. She had to have dressed him herself. They were both smiling.

"Breakfast is served," Kethlyn said.

Scotty and I stood and followed our children into the dining room, to find the table set more or less properly, with fruit salad, scrambled eggs, grits, and toast on the plates. I was amazed. The fruit was cut—in big chunks, but they had cut it up—and the salad contained everything in the produce drawer: apple, pear, grapes, carrots, and celery. The eggs were even cooked well. They didn't manage the grits too well, but we did fine with the rest. I could see from Scotty's face that he was as overjoyed as I was. We were both beaming.

"This is wonderful, Kethlyn," I said. "What gave you guys the idea to make breakfast?"

She shrugged. "I just wanted to."

"Well, Bud," Scotty said, "I'm proud of you both. You did a real good job."

Here was Kethlyn, already being decisive, taking risks, and leading her little brother, and Kheaton, so young and already wanting to be a helper.

After breakfast, we carried our dishes into the kitchen. It was completely trashed. Every chair from the kitchen table had been pushed up against the counters. All the knives were out, and there was food on every surface. But there was no fire, and nothing was broken.

This is possibly my favorite story about my kids. I smile every time I remember that morning. Both Scotty and I enjoy cooking and entertaining, and both the kids had helped us many times. But we hadn't realized how much they had learned. I'm proud of Kethlyn and Kheaton, and I'm grateful that we were able to impart the values we felt were important for our kids' success. As parents, Scotty and I would repeat this moment many times—standing by, sometimes anxiously, watching our children grow into themselves. This is what it feels like to live your values—you have to trust yourself, even when doing so feels risky. It wasn't easy to stay there at the top of the steps—I know many parents who would disagree with our choice—but it was a choice that fit our values. We took a risk, and the rewards were great. It would not be the last time our family took risks together.

22

Forget About Work/Life Balance

Okay, let's get this out of the way: I hate the phrase *work/life balance*. The word *balance* implies a fixed equilibrium, a two-arm scale with equal weight on each arm. That's just not how life works. If we hold balance as the standard for success, we're bound to feel like we're failing. We need a different metaphor, one that can hold all the complexities and overlapping responsibilities of career, family relationships, friendships, self-care—whatever components you choose to include in your life. That's why I prefer the term *work/life integration*.

How do I really make my life work? I don't put on one hat and take off another; I wear all my hats, all the time: Shellye the CEO, Shellye the mom, Shellye the wife, the friend, the volunteer, the mentor, the mentee. Of course, in any given moment, I'm focusing my attention in one particular area, but I'm always trying to integrate everything that makes me myself, at all times. You can do this, too.

Whatever your goals—whether you want to run a company, go back to school, put your kids through school, retire early, change careers—you are in control of how you integrate your life in order to make it happen. Look at your options. Play with the possibilities. Where can you make room for the things that are currently a priority? Who can help you get it done? How can you accomplish multiple things in one action?

While the standard of *balance* can feel limiting (if not impossible), the concept of *integration* is empowering—it's an invitation to get creative. For example, I found it challenging to integrate time for friends and networking into my busy schedule, but I learned a few tricks. I could exercise with a friend, take the kids to the park with other mothers, or invite people over for potluck dinner and a movie or card playing. At work, on occasion I'd leverage lunchtime to network, or I'd take a walking meeting to combine work and exercise. When Scotty and I did go out, we'd often invite others, combining socializing and networking. I continue these practices to this day. Scotty and I rarely go to our favorite dance performances with fewer than twenty friends.

Likewise, I make time for small luxuries that matter to me by integrating them into other activities. For example, I like to bake, and Scotty and I really enjoy apple pies. Sometimes I'd invite my neighbor over, and together we would make enough filling for ten pies. She would take home half, and I'd bake one pie and put the filling for the other four in the freezer. We cooked and socialized together.

It's amazing what you can do when you operate from a "no time wasted" position. I didn't always have time or money for the nail salon, but I like to have my nails done. So I started putting polish on my nails in the car before I left for work. I'd drive with the air blowing in the car or the windows down, and by the time I got to the office, my nails were dry. Similarly, I prioritize exercise, and I also like to keep up with the news, so I read or listen to podcasts while I'm doing cardio at the gym. No wasted time.

I know what you're thinking: Surely, you can't do *everything* you want to do. You must make *some* sacrifices. As I've said before, as much as I don't like the phrase *work/life balance*, I don't like when people talk about "sacrificing" one part of their lives for another. To me, the word *sacrifice* implies a sense of loss that engenders guilt. If you're giving "too much" time to work, you feel guilty about giving "not enough" time at home. Or vice versa. Worse, a "sacrifice" typically refers to giving something up for someone else—your boss, your team, your spouse, your child, your mother—which further implies you did it only to fulfill someone else's needs, not your own. In this sense, the idea of "making sacrifices" paints you as a victim—someone who had to give up what she really wants, in service of someone else.

Remember that story about my mom getting the smallest piece of pie? Well, she also got a horse. Like Mom, I believe in making choices, not sacrifices. Choices I own—no one else to blame, no guilt placed.

Let's go back to our decision to hire a nanny, which allowed me to perform better at work without worrying about whether our baby was okay. Scotty and I budgeted for a nanny before I got pregnant, before we even got married. We created financial flexibility by saving money on some things that weren't strictly necessary, and we used that financial flexibility to get help where we needed it. At this stage in our lives, we didn't take fancy vacations, and date nights were usually pizza and wine at our favorite Italian restaurant. We bought a smaller house, farther from work, and we drove the long commute in older cars than we could have been driving if we didn't have a nanny to pay. But these adjustments were worth it, because our kids were healthy, we felt less stress, and we even had more quality time with our kids in the evening, because some of the household tasks had been taken care of already.

Of course, I'm not saying that every mom should stay in the workforce and hire a nanny. I'm saying you should choose the life you want and make decisions to support that lifestyle. Of all the possible ways we could have shaped our lives, this is what Scotty and I wanted to do. We supported our decision by making conscious choices. This wasn't a sacrifice. It was a choice.

That's the message I hope to pass on to the next generation: You don't have to apologize for being who you are and making the choices you make. You deserve the chance to shape the life you want and to celebrate and enjoy the life you've created. Your destiny is yours, and if you move toward it without shame, you can keep every ounce of your self-respect while attaining what you desire.

From childhood, my parents taught me that saying yes to one thing is saying no to another. This is true not only for how you spend your money, but also for how you spend your time. Both resources are finite, so you've got to budget. If you want to invest in a good education, you will probably trade off some social opportunities. If you want children, you will give up some sleep. If you want a challenging career, your time for certain aspects of home life will be limited. (If you asked me, I'd say I didn't miss doing the laundry; I did miss the sleep.)

My point is this: You are, right this minute, fully empowered to make your own decisions about what you want and what will make you happy. You are fully empowered to make the choices you need to make to support that life—integrating your activities, budgeting your money and time. You don't have to "go with the flow." You don't have to follow anybody else's rules. Begin now to write your own. I custom-designed a life plan that would make me fulfilled. I strategized for it, choosing what I was willing to do, choosing the trade-offs I was willing to make, and I went after the life I wanted, unapologetically. You can, too.

23

Manage Your Own Career

I had to quit my job to get the job I wanted. That was a learning experience, all right.

I was in my late twenties, approaching thirty, and that was important to me. According to my self-imposed timeline, if I was going to be the CEO of IBM, I needed to be a branch manager by the time I turned thirty. I was on track. My ratings and performance were strong, but I had at least one step to take before I could be considered for branch manager. I needed to become a marketing manager, and if I didn't get that job soon, I'd risk missing my objective for age thirty.

For a while now, I had been sharing with my boss my desire to get a marketing manager job. He had agreed that it was the next step, but no opportunities were coming my way. So I went to see him again.

I found the door to his office open, the afternoon sun

casting a beam of light across his desk, where he was seated, flipping through paperwork. I knocked on the open door to get his attention and asked if he had a few minutes to talk. He waved me in.

"As we've discussed, I'd like to be considered for a marketing manager role," I said. I had learned by now that you have to tell people what you're after.

He sighed—not a good sign. "Well, that's going to be a stretch right now."

My heart plummeted. "Why do you say that?"

"Well, IBM is tightening its belt. You know they've reorganized and closed some branches and had people retire early. That means there are fewer branches, so there are fewer opportunities to get a marketing manager position."

"I understand, but don't you think I'd be a good candidate nonetheless?"

"Shellye," he said, "you're doing great. Your performance is excellent. But there just aren't opportunities to advance right now."

Okay. This was not the news I needed to hear. So that night, I decided to talk it over with Scotty.

Once the kids were in bed and things were quiet, I poured myself a glass of wine and sat down next to him on the couch, handing him a beer.

He raised an eyebrow. "What's the occasion?"

So I told him about my conversation with my boss. He listened with a furrowed brow. We both knew things were changing at IBM, and neither of us liked it.

"So, then, what are you going to do?" he asked.

I sighed. "I don't know. You know I want to run a business, not just work at one. I need to be able to move up as rapidly as possible. I have the skill, I'm being told I have the capabilities, I'm delivering—so this is an IBM issue, right?"

"Right." He stared directly at me. "It's not you, it's them." My husband, always building my confidence.

I ran a finger around the rim of my glass, thinking. "Well then . . ." I inhaled deeply.

Scotty finished my thought: "Maybe you need to go outside IBM."

This was no small consideration. After all, I'd worked for IBM, a company known in the industry as Big Blue, since high school. My father had worked for IBM his entire adult life. I used to joke that if you cut me, I'd bleed blue. But if IBM didn't have the opportunities I wanted, I wasn't going to let company loyalty get in the way of my goals. So I found another company that offered the position I wanted. I interviewed, and I got the job.

With that job offer in my pocket, I dressed in one of my sharpest outfits, walked into the company I loved—the place I had hoped to helm one day—and I resigned.

"What do you mean?" my boss asked. "You're leaving? You can't resign."

I didn't say anything. I knew I was one of their best employees. My boss's face told me the rest of what I needed to know.

He leaned his elbows on the desk and looked me in the eyes. "Shellye, why are you quitting?"

"Well, you told me there weren't any opportunities for promotion coming up. So I found another job that would be a step up. You know I have ambitions, and it breaks my heart that I can't achieve them here."

He shook his head. "Shellye, I'm going to ask you to give me a chance here. Let me see what I can do."

A few days later, I got the commitment for the promotion. I was now a marketing manager, right on my self-made timeline, and right there at IBM.

That was the first big lesson I learned about advancing in the corporate world: You can't wait for someone else to hand you an opportunity; you have to manage your own career.

24

Tell People What You Want

The next lesson came a few years later, when I was hoping for my promotion to branch manager level. By this time, I'd become pretty good at telling people what I wanted to do. I had discussed my ambitions with my boss again, but nothing was happening. It felt like things were stalled. *What am I doing wrong?* I wondered. *I'm ready for that next title. Why am I not being considered for anything?*

Since I wasn't getting anywhere with my boss, I decided to have a conversation with my boss's boss—what's called a skip-level interview. The meeting was scheduled a few weeks out, so I had time to rehearse the best way to communicate what I wanted. When the time came around, I presented my case. I explained what I had achieved in my current position, and how that made me a strong candidate for the position I wanted. I felt the conversation was going well—until I told my boss's boss I wanted to be a branch manager.

He cleared his throat. "Yes, Shellye," he said. "You're certainly a strong candidate, but we just don't have many roles like that in the Harrisburg area."

"Well, yes, but I'm willing to move," I said.

He raised his eyebrows and looked at me incredulously. "You're willing to move? We didn't think you'd want to."

I was nonplussed. I had already moved twice in my career, and I had told my boss that I was willing to move again. Why hadn't he passed on this important information? "Yes, absolutely, I'm willing to move."

"Well, in that case, we'll try to find an opportunity you can compete for," he said. "Thank you for clearing that up."

I'll never know why that information had not been communicated correctly. I won't venture to guess. But after that conversation, lo and behold, an opportunity came up in Maryland, and I had the chance to compete. I got the job.

There's some conventional wisdom in the professional world about why women don't get promoted. More or less, it boils down to "women don't ask for what they want." The reality, however, is much more complex.

In 2016, the *Women in the Workplace* study found that women do ask for what they want—a big change since the early years of my own career.[15] This is positive progress, but there's a catch: Women who negotiate are 30 percent more likely than men to be told they are too "aggressive," "bossy," or "intimidating." Moreover, women receive less informal feedback from their supervisors, which suggests a communication disconnect, not to mention a paradox: Women are told, simultaneously, to ask for what we want *and* to stop pushing. Interestingly, both those pieces of feedback turn the responsibility back to us, suggesting it's our fault if we have difficulty getting opportunities. Meanwhile, we are hard pressed to get constructive feedback on how to become that ideal assertive yet gentle employee. Could it be that this ideal is not realistic? Research shows that women still encounter unrealistic expectations in the workplace.[16] Most likely, neither women nor men are fully aware of how those expectations are playing out in our interactions.

I cannot say I have a solution to this issue, but I can tell you what has worked for me: Not only have I learned to tell people what I want, but I've also learned to tell *everyone* what I want. When I have a goal, I put it out in the open, and it becomes a part of my identity. Broadcast your intentions! You never know who is listening, who might have a connection—or conversely, who might have their own reasons to withhold information. The more people who know what you want, the more likely you are to get an opportunity.

It takes some guts to tell everyone what you want. It does feel risky. But you have to learn to take those risks. I have a mantra in these situations. I ask myself:

What's the worst that can happen?

Can I live with it if the worst does happen?

Usually, when it comes to asking for what I want, the worst that can happen is I might get told no, and I can live with that. I have found that the benefits of broadcasting my intentions far outweigh the discomfort of hearing no.

25

Let It Go

Remember I told you that IBM was downsizing? Well, for Scotty, that looked like an opportunity. He was a second-line manager himself, meaning he had managers reporting to him. One day, he received a list of names—people who were being offered an early retirement in his organization with a generous package. It was the second time IBM had downsized, and this was their way to avoid layoffs. Scotty got a chance to look at the package ahead of time, and he immediately picked up the phone and called me. "Shellye," he said, "this thing has my name all over it."

The timing couldn't have been better. Kethlyn was just about to start first grade. We were ready to begin the next phase of our life plan, with Scotty as the at-home dad, and this offer would give us a little extra in funds to get us going. Scotty had been working at IBM for more than twenty years by then, so his retirement payout was good. He could pick up some consulting work and move into a home office. It was time for my husband to take a risk, and to my great pleasure, he was not at all apprehensive about it. Scotty and I had always been equal partners, and we always knew the game plan. It was simply time to execute the next step.

By the time I got the job in Silver Springs, Maryland, Scotty was ready to retire fully. Since we were relocating, we also took the opportunity to downsize and tighten our budget to live on a single income. We got a smaller house, traded in our leased cars for used vehicles with lower payments, and of course, we said goodbye to our nanny.

Everything was working out fine, except for one thing, one major thing: When the nanny left, I started treating Scotty like he was taking over that job. I meant to be helpful, telling him how things should be done, giving him a few tasks for each day, just as I had done with the nanny. But it didn't go over very well.

As I swept into the kitchen dressed in my IBM suit and heels, I opened the refrigerator, grabbed a yogurt and an apple, and stuffed them into my briefcase. The kids sat at the breakfast table, drinking juice. Scotty stood at the stove, spooning grits onto the kids' plates, alongside scrambled eggs and sausage. On the counter, open lunch boxes waited to be filled. "Scotty, don't forget that Kethlyn likes her sandwiches cut into quarters," I said.

He nodded.

"And you don't need to do laundry every day, it can wait," I noted.

"I don't like piles of dirty clothes in the laundry room," he explained, irritation edging his voice.

"But it just wastes water," I countered, "washing partial loads." Scotty shook his head.

"By the way," I added, assessing the haphazard stacks of mail, paperwork, and miscellaneous junk piled in a corner of the counter, "can you clear off the kitchen counter this afternoon? It's really gotten out of hand." I bent down to kiss the kids goodbye and walked out the door.

Well, after a few more mornings of my "helpful" instructions, Scotty had had enough. "Shellye," he said firmly, "if I'm going to do this job, then *I'm* going to do it. If you want to be in charge of how things get done, then I'm not doing it."

That was a tense conversation, but I got it: I couldn't just tell him what to do. Changing that behavior was surprisingly difficult, but over the course of several months, I worked on tapping into what I had learned from my counselor about letting things go. Scotty was amazingly clean, but clutter didn't bother him too much. I was just the opposite. I liked everything in its place, but I could live with a little dust. *So maybe Scotty lets things get a little messier than I like them. Nothing is dirty or unsafe, so I have to let it go.* As I thought this through, I asked myself: *Why am I so particular about things being neat? Why do I feel it's so important? Why is it so hard for me to abdicate that responsibility?*

You know when people come over to your house for the first time? They step in, they look around, and they say, "Oh, Shellye, what a nice house you have." Not "Scotty," but "Shellye." I was the one receiving comments about the appearance of my home, the appearance and manners of my children, even my husband's appearance and grooming. It's just how people think. The encoded implication is that everything to do with keeping things neat and clean and orderly is the woman's responsibility.

I had internalized that expectation and felt judged, like so many people do: If the house was messy, it reflected poorly on me. For so many reasons, I had to let that go. Somebody else was in charge now, and I had other responsibilities.

I have a photo—one of Kethlyn's school portraits—that's the perfect symbol of what this letting-go process meant for us. For the photo, her two braids were supposed to be pinned to the top of her head like a little crown. But one had come unpinned and fallen down. So when her picture was taken, she had one braid up, one braid down and unraveling. That's because Scotty had taken over the job of doing Kethlyn's hair before school, and on the day the photo was taken, he hadn't quite mastered the bobby pins yet. Scotty was learning, and that wasn't the only time Kethlyn's braids were crooked. But instead of fixing it for him or trying to take over the responsibility, I just let him learn. I stepped back, and my husband stepped in, and we still have that photo proudly hanging on the wall.

26

Every Move Is "Our" Move

My new job brought me up to the level I'd call pre-executive. I was just one move away from an executive-level position now. Of course, as I've mentioned, ambition is not just about climbing the ladder. You have to do the best you can at the job you're in; otherwise you won't have opportunities for advancement. I concentrated hard on my performance, and I developed some strong mentorship relationships with people above and below me on that ladder. I was getting good performance reviews, good support, good feedback, and I was telling everyone that I wanted an executive job. After a few years in Maryland, I finally got my shot. A position opened up in New York: global head of market management for the small and medium business segment of IBM, working for Robin Sternbergh. I went for it, and I got it. So the family moved to Connecticut, and I began commuting to New York.

Now that I had my executive position, I knew what had to happen next. I did my homework, and I discovered something pretty extraordinary about IBM's top executives: Every single one of them had taken an international assignment at one point. Even more interesting: Nearly all of the line executives who worked for the CEO had been stationed in Japan working in the Asia Pacific region. "That's not obvious," I thought. "Asia Pacific was not one of the largest regions." My next move was crystal clear: I had to find a job in IBM's headquarters in Tokyo. My strategy, by this time, was consistent. I kept my head in the game and continued to do my job as well as I could. I developed my relationships with mentors, with higher-ups, as well as with my own team. And I told absolutely everyone that I wanted an executive assignment in Japan.

Japan assignments were generally temporary, and there weren't many expat positions. Fortunately, an executive whom I had gotten to know when I worked in Maryland, Tim McChristian, was promoted to a job in Japan. Although I had never worked for Tim, I had stayed in touch; and as it turned out, when we moved to Connecticut, we moved into the same neighborhood he lived in. Broadcasting my desire to work in Japan paid off. Tim asked me to sign on as his general manager for direct marketing, and I eagerly accepted.

There was just one issue: The family was coming with me. Were we ready to spend the next few years in a foreign country? Kethlyn in particular was nonplussed. She was in seventh grade now, old and wise enough to be tired of moving around. The last time we had moved, from Maryland to Connecticut, she understandably had experienced it as a personal tragedy. She had begun to cry as soon as we told her, and that had made Kheaton cry, too. Their misery was heartbreaking. This time, we'd be making a bigger move, into a very different situation, and I'd be pulling both kids away from good friends. Scotty and I knew we needed to help them feel confident about it. So we decided to try something different. Instead of sitting both children down to tell them about our plan, we told Kethlyn privately. As expected, she was heartbroken. We consoled her as best we could, emphasizing the great adventure we'd have, and I promised her that Japan was only temporary. Then we sent her off to process the news, which for a preteen means talking to her friends.

To our great pleasure, our daughter returned two hours later with what almost looked like a smile on her face. "Okay," she said. "I've dealt with it. When do we move?"

"That's great, Kethlyn," I said as we hugged. "So if you're ready, we want you to go tell your brother that we're moving. He looks up to you. This will be a great opportunity for both of you."

A few minutes later, here came Kheaton, bopping in with a huge grin on his face. "Mom! Dad! We're moving to Japan?"

Older siblings are role models to the younger ones, and Kheaton took his cues from Kethlyn in those years, as he will readily admit. She was a good role model, and in this case, her ability to process and adapt quickly to change helped Kheaton feel confident and optimistic. Already, our daughter was stronger than we expected.

⌢

I could write a book just on the lessons we learned in Tokyo— perhaps another time. I will say that we had a blast there as a family, and that I enjoyed the work, too.

For us as a family, the most impactful cultural difference was the near-complete absence of crime. In a city of ten million people, children are safe to walk downtown, ride the subways, or catch a cab by themselves. So our kids did. This was a confidence-building experience for them. Soon they would make friends at school, and we wouldn't see them quite as much. Often, Scotty and I found ourselves with free evenings, and we spent them exploring the city, going to concerts, and doing things we'd never have had time for in the States.

Freedom wasn't the only thing we gained. As I was building skills and experiences at work, so was my family at home. We lived in Nishi Azabu, right off Roppongi-dori, in the heart of Tokyo. This was equivalent to living in Manhattan. By Japanese standards, our apartment was huge at 1,100 square feet. Our kids were enrolled in the Tokyo American School, which catered to children of expatriates. IBM provided quite a bit of support, such as membership in the Tokyo American Club, which was the social center for American expats. They also provided Japanese lessons for Scotty. The first lesson went fine until the teacher outlined the homework. "Homework? I'm not doing any home-work," he said. And that was the end of his lessons. As he ran his daily errands, he became quite adept at pantomiming to communicate what he needed. Every so often it would backfire, though. One time, he tried to buy the equivalent of Jet-Dry dishwasher rinse agent. Well, whatever he put in the dishwasher caused it to erupt with never-ending suds that flooded the kitchen, hallway, and part of the main room. When this happened, I didn't say a word. Just like our kids, Scotty was "doing Tokyo" his way.

Speaking of the kids, on a Saturday a few weeks after school started, Kheaton was home watching one of the few English-language stations on TV. Kethlyn, the more outgoing child, was visiting a new friend. I asked Kheaton how he was doing in fifth grade. His school was very diverse, with students from over thirty-five countries. "Fine, Mom," he said, looking up.

"No, Kheaton, really," I said, sliding next to him on the futon. "Things are very different here. How are you truly feeling?"

"Mom," he said, shaking his head at me, almost condescending, "the kids are the same; they just have accents."

I broke into a big smile. "If that is all you learn while we are here in Tokyo, that is fine with me," I said, pulling him into a hug.

Though this leap forward in my career meant big changes for the whole family, each of us benefited in our own ways as well, individually and together.

27

Your Challenges Are Your Strengths

IBM spent a lot of money to send people to places like Japan, in particular subsidizing family expenses and education. Because it was expensive, they invested exclusively in their "high-potential" employees. Based on performance, support, and culture fit, senior management expected that these employees would rise to high levels in the company.

Just as Steve Jobs, in his turtleneck and wire-rimmed glasses, became a prototype of the successful Silicon Valley entrepreneur, IBM had its own prototypical high-potential employee in the 1980s and '90s. They looked like this: men in dark suits, white shirts, a tie, and wing-tipped shoes. Many were golfers or athletes who projected confidence in the way they carried themselves. I was not necessarily that type. In fact, I was the first African American female executive ever to be sent on an international assignment.

Before I left for Japan, I spoke with my current boss, an Australian who had worked for many years in Asia. He gave me some advice that had me a little worried.

"Shellye," he explained, "in Japanese culture, there are three qualities that cause people to treat you with respect and help you succeed."

I nodded. This was exactly what I needed to know. "Tell me."

"The first is wisdom, a nice term for being old. But you don't have that one going for you."

I was thirty-six. Strike one.

"Second," he continued, "being male. Again, you don't have it." He cleared his throat. "The third quality is intelligence. You've got that, but it's the only one, and you better maximize it." He looked right at me. "I have faith in you."

But my own faith was a little shaken. *I worked hard to get to this opportunity in Japan, and now I'm being told the deck is stacked against me . . . again?*

So I did what I always do when the odds aren't in my favor: I did my homework. I bought books on doing business in Japan. I talked to people who had worked there in the past. I did as much research as I could before I got on the plane, and I arrived in Japan ready to serve as the general manager for direct marketing for Asia Pacific. When I started working with my new team, I quickly discovered a detail my boss had missed—one I was uniquely qualified to see.

I worked with many wonderful people who gave their all and did their best work at IBM, but I noticed a particular blind spot among the more ambitious set, IBM's high-potential "type." When they took a new assignment, they assumed that everything they'd done—their accomplishments and accolades, the reputations they'd developed—came with them. In other words, they presumed they were going to be treated with respect. Not so for me. As a young African American woman, I was accustomed to *earning* respect. Whenever I got a promotion or a new job, I walked into it understanding that people likely would assume I was not quite qualified or not quite ready. I presumed I needed to establish relationships and credibility, to develop a reputation, to prove myself. In other words, I may not have had age and maleness working for me, but because I had spent so much of my life outside my comfort zone, I had developed team-building skills and the ability to make alliances quickly. These skills came into play when I gave my first presentation to my Japanese team.

My objective was to communicate our strategy to grow the business. I spent a fair amount of time crafting my message and preparing. While the Japanese executives spoke English fairly well, the rank-and-file employees' English skills were mixed. I wanted to make sure everyone could understand what I was communicating, so I had my slides translated into Japanese. Doing so just made sense. After all, I didn't have to understand my slides; I already knew what I planned to say.

When I arrived at the IBM Japan building, I was formally greeted and escorted to the conference room where hundreds of people were finding their seats. In the front of the room stood an overhead projector reflecting a slide that read "Japan Direct Marketing." Frankly, I was a little nervous as I was being introduced to members of the team. I grasped only a small subset of the names I was hearing—Takahashi-san, Watanabe-san, Akiyama-san . . . Finally, it was time to start.

When I put the first slide up, I heard an audible murmur

throughout the room. My first thought: *Oh no! The translator must have done something terribly wrong.* I later found out the true cause of the ruckus. In all the years IBM executives had been making presentations in Japan, no American executive had provided slides written 100 percent in Japanese, at least not that the people in that room could recall. The Americans lived inside an English-only zone, and I had broken that invisible barrier.

When I was facing the challenges and trials of my youth, I never realized the strengths I was developing. Beyond my innate ambition and my education, I had learned how to get people to like me—whether they thought they wanted to or not—by being empathetic and helpful. I had discovered the power of alliances and teams—by working together, you accomplish more. Sure, as a young African American woman, I did not have many cultural advantages going into Japan's business environment, but in the end, I developed a good reputation and built successful teams. When my stateside colleagues asked me how I did it, I had to be honest. "I've always been an outsider," I explained. "Everywhere I went, I had to learn how to get along with all types of people and earn their respect."

I was better prepared for that job in Japan than I had realized—better prepared, in fact, than many of those prototypical IBM employees. This experience reinforced my parents' message: Being in the minority doesn't have to hold you back. In fact, it can be an advantage. The hard-won lessons you learn while meeting life's challenges? If you leverage them right, they become your secret weapons.

PART FOUR

SWERVE

28

Move Around the Blocks You Can't Remove

I never did become CEO of IBM. Once again, I had to quit my job to get the job I wanted—but this time, I never went back.

It was 1999, and we were living in Japan. I had recently been promoted to vice president and general manager for public sector industry for Asia Pacific, a multibillion-dollar division, when Lou Gerstner, IBM's CEO at that time, made a trip to Tokyo. Many of my peers were invited to have one-on-one meetings with Lou. Despite having the best year-over-year revenue growth for the previous two quarters, I received no such invitation. I was definitely disappointed, but when I told Scotty, he was furious. "How can that be?" he fumed. "As good as you are, why weren't you the first one he sat down with? This isn't right…," and on and on he went. Scotty's always been my biggest support and cheerleader, but his rant did something else for me: It helped me step back and see that this was more than just a slight.

This wasn't the first clue that I wasn't getting my due at IBM. I was ranked highly in terms of my performance—close to the top of the yearly rankings, not just in Japan, but globally. Yet I was pretty sure I wasn't earning the salary many of my colleagues were getting. I wasn't a mercenary about money, but my family had made many hard choices to support my career, so it was important to me to be paid a competitive market rate. And I wasn't, despite raising the issue multiple times over the years.

Scotty and I discussed my situation over the coming weeks. I was really struggling. I always pictured myself working for IBM and running it. Due to all the relocations, and Scotty's career in IBM, most of our friends were IBMers. I actually felt disloyal, and even guilty, just thinking about leaving the company and leaving them. In many ways, I grew up in IBM.

I went through an emotional roller coaster during this period. One minute I'd be angry with IBM for letting me down and putting me in this position, and then I'd be sad and unsure, thinking about leaving my IBM "family." I'd try to rationalize that perhaps I was misreading the cues and hadn't done all in my power to position myself properly and convince myself I should stay. After all, it would be easier and more comfortable just to stay. But we kept coming back to my goal to be CEO, and the fact that I deserved to be paid fairly.

Ultimately, we decided it was time to get my seat at the table and to be paid fairly for it. If IBM wasn't going to pay me to sit at the IBM table, I would just have to find another one. I held tight to my goal of becoming a CEO, and I looked for the best next step to support that goal.

Though I'd been running a multibillion-dollar business for IBM, research had taught me that people who leave a large company to run a smaller one often struggle and stumble in the new environment. As a minority female, I knew that I didn't have as many chances at bat as the guys, so I wanted to increase my odds for success. Before going after a CEO job, I decided I needed to learn what was so different about smaller companies. I resigned from IBM and moved the family to Dallas, where I became president of Blockbuster.com and doubled my income.

As I said, this was 1999, and the internet was new on the business scene. Blockbuster was just getting its website running, and I was head of a relatively independent division within the company. We launched Blockbuster.com initially to offer information about movies, the industry, and Blockbuster stores, and to sell videos and movie paraphernalia. The ultimate vision was to make it a web portal for downloading movies. I was excited about the challenge, excited to be working in such a vibrant sector with so much potential for growth. My kids loved all the free videos, too.

It wasn't long before an even bigger opportunity came along. I was approached by Reed Hastings, head of Netflix. At the time, Netflix had terrific technology, but they didn't have relationships with the movie studios and content companies. Blockbuster didn't have the technology, but it had everything else: relationships with all the movie studios and theaters, and a nationally dominant network with a very active customer base. Hastings thought that Netflix and Blockbuster could combine under the Blockbuster.com brand and conquer the world. I thought he was absolutely right.

Reed and a couple of his team members flew to Dallas to make the pitch. After that meeting, my boss made it clear to the executive team that he would not support the proposal.

"Netflix is nothing," he said. "They'll never get off the ground, and if they ever turn into anything, then we will buy them." Discussion closed.

I couldn't believe what I was hearing. We had a chance to dominate the world of rental movies and ultimately streaming, to step into the future. But Blockbuster leadership could not be convinced. I was less than eight months into my tenure. I tried to focus on building BB.com and developing new offerings like reserving a movie online and picking it up in the store, but as far as I was concerned, the writing was on the wall. Based on the Blockbuster strategy, I knew this was not the company for me.

Sometimes you come upon roadblocks you just can't move, so you need to go around them.

At this time, Silicon Valley was all over the news. California was experiencing a second "gold rush," but this time tech was gold, and people from all over the world were flocking to Silicon Valley to pan for internet success.

"Scotty, I think I'm done at Blockbuster," I said one night to my dear, patient husband. "I think I need to go to Silicon Valley and be where the action is." And of course, he supported my decision.

29

Make the Right Choice at the Right Time

During my thirties, my family moved several times, and every time I immediately got to work laying down roots in our new town, just as my mother had done when I was a child. While my mom's strategy was to walk us kids around the neighborhood to make introductions, I had my own hack for getting to know our neighbors. If you've ever moved, you know it takes a while to unpack and get settled, right? Meanwhile, inevitably there's some simple item you really need but can't find, right? Well, whether I could find what I needed or not, I would knock on the door of a neighbor, introduce myself as a member of the family that just moved in, and ask to borrow something: a hammer, a screwdriver, a stapler . . . It didn't matter. It was just an excuse to connect. Then I would connect again when I returned it. Then Scotty and I would enact a follow-up strategy—we'd throw a party within sixty days of moving in. The party did two things for us: It set a deadline for getting things out of boxes, and it served as a follow-up to those initial connections with our neighbors. We would invite whomever we'd met and liked in those first sixty days. These eclectic gatherings kicked off our social interactions, as some guests would return the favor and invite us to an event at their homes.

Our parties kicked off our socializing as a family, but each family member had their own adjusting to do each time we moved. In Dallas, at first, Kheaton's friends thought it was odd that his dad didn't work. But it didn't take long before they found out what fun Scotty could be. After a few afternoons of basketball and dinner at our house, Kheaton's friends came to think of Scotty as the coolest dad around.

Let's talk for just a minute about the reality of Scotty, an at-home dad, an ex–football player in his fifties, waiting to pick up the kids after school or a dance class, with the moms of our Dallas suburb. Just picture that: Scotty, still very much in shape at six foot two, two hundred pounds of lean muscle, broad shoulders, and long legs, standing among these women who could have been cast members in *The Real Housewives*. Luckily, Scotty is outgoing, talkative, funny, and charming. If he encountered any awkwardness, he handled it up front.

One of Scotty's favorite stories from those early days in Dallas is about a phone call he got from the mother of one of Kheaton's football teammates. Scotty had spoken to her before, but only with that arm's-length Southern politeness.

"What can I do for you, ma'am?" he asked her.

"Well, um—well, I am calling you because my son told me I had to," she confessed. "He wanted me to find out how you get Kheaton's uniform so clean and white."

"Oh, we've got a secret concoction for that," Scotty said.

The secret had been handed down from my mother, and Scotty shared it: Put the ends of bath soap bars in a glass jar, add two tablespoons of ammonia and one cup of water, and keep it sealed in the laundry room. When you have a stain, dip an old toothbrush in the jar and rub it against the soap. Scrub the stain with the toothbrush, and launder as usual. She thanked him for the tip, and from then on, their relationship was that much warmer.

While Scotty and Kheaton were finding their way into our Dallas community, Kethlyn was doing the same, in her own way. She was growing into a bright, driven young woman. I saw so much of myself in her, and I still do. But all was not perfect in her world. I don't think Scotty or I realized how much it was affecting our daughter to move every few years. Certainly, I can identify with the disruption, having moved plenty of times in my own childhood. But I had my sisters and my mother; Kethlyn had to say goodbye to all her girlfriends every time we left. Repeat relocations thrust her into new situations where she would modify her personality in order to fit in, mirroring the language, interests, and behavior of the people around her. I think she lost a little bit of herself along the way. Kethlyn was very clear with us that she hated moving, but we kept moving anyway. Talk about a blow to the self-esteem. It's hard to feel self-sufficient when your most fervent wishes are ignored. At least, that's how it felt from her perspective.

This came to a head in middle school, when we moved to Japan. Kethlyn took that move in stride, I thought, but later I learned it was a real injury to her. At the time, she was going into eighth grade, and all she really wanted to do was finish middle school with her friends. She wanted close, long-term friends, and we kept ripping her away from them. When we made the move from Japan to Dallas, I kept that in mind. In her freshman year of high school, Scotty and I made Kethlyn a promise: We would not force her to move again during high school, if she didn't want to leave.

Speaking of school, from the time our kids started elementary school, with each move our family made, Scotty and I had adopted my parents' strategy of moving into the best school districts we could manage. In Dallas, this meant our neighborhood was, as we used to say (between ourselves), full of executives and trust-fund babies. This also meant that, culturally and racially, it was fairly homogeneous. Actually, it was so homogeneous that Kethlyn was the only black girl in her entire high school. The whole school. *Oh my God! She's just moved from a foreign country, and instead of feeling at home and comfortable, she still feels like one of a kind.* I couldn't help but remember what that had felt like for me. The parallel was too neat, and I felt her apprehension in my heart.

One weekend, not long after we moved to Dallas, I decided to ask Kethlyn about it. "Kethlyn, what do you think about your new school so far? Are you meeting anybody interesting?"

She slumped visibly. "Ugh. No. Mom, there is nobody at that school I can relate to."

I cringed on the inside but tried to smile comfortingly. "Really, Doll? Not one person?"

"No, Mom, it's awful. Everybody's running around with their Prada purses and their designer shoes, and I can't even talk to them. There's no way I'm going to fit in here. I hate it here!"

I believed her. Kethlyn had shared that people were telling

her she was the only black person they had ever met. I had seen our neighbors' houses and the cars parked in front of the school. But I had also lived through this before, and I knew what to say. I took Kethlyn's hand and squeezed it. "Listen, Doll, I know it feels that way to you right now, and I believe what you're saying. But those girls you're seeing are the ones who want to be seen. That's why they're showing off their wealth, to be noticed. If you look a little deeper, I promise you, you'll see not everybody's like that."

She scoffed.

"Kethlyn, I am serious. I know there are people at your school who share your values and priorities. Not everybody at that school is exactly the same. Look deeper, and you will find people like you. I promise."

Kethlyn, bless her heart, took my word for it. She went back to school and tried. She earned a spot on the drill team (which was a big deal in Texas), and she became its first-ever black lieutenant. She joined Habitat for Humanity, performed in a few school plays, and yes, she found lifelong friends.

As for Kheaton, he was (and still is) a very fun and likeable guy. He's never had trouble getting along with people. But as he was growing into himself, he was developing a certain— not cynicism, exactly, but a feeling that he didn't want other people to tell him what was important and what wasn't. This applied to schoolwork in particular. He simply didn't want to do it. Kheaton's teachers told us he was intelligent but he didn't apply himself. He was entering a danger zone, with poor grades and frustrated instructors. We were frustrated, too—especially because Kheaton excelled in all his extracurricular activities— but we just couldn't convince him to do his schoolwork.

"This doesn't matter," he would say. "Why should I do this busywork?"

"Because, Bud," Scotty told him again and again, "you have to get the grades so you can get into a college, get a degree, and then you can do whatever you want in life."

"But what if what I want to do doesn't have anything to do with college?" he'd ask.

For us, the answer was obvious: You go to college and get the degree so you have *options*, so you can choose any path you want. But this did not convince our son. After much discussion and hand-wringing, Scotty and I made the choice to send Kheaton to a military boot camp–style facility over the summer. We thought maybe the structure and the emphasis on working toward a goal would be invigorating for him. Of course, he thought it was torture.

"Do you want to go back again?" I asked.

"No!"

"Okay, then in that case it's totally up to you. I'm not asking you to get straight As, Kheat. Just do your work."

After that summer, he did. He never went back to that camp again, and miraculously, he doesn't seem to have hard feelings toward us for sending him. In fact, he once thanked us for being patient with him during that time. I feel the same gratitude toward him for being patient with us.

Even before we became parents, Scotty and I had identified three main qualities we wanted to help our future children develop: self-sufficiency, confidence, and caring for others. I could see these qualities growing in Kethlyn and Kheaton. Finally, it seemed like everyone had settled into life in Dallas.

And then I decided to move to California.

This was the last straw for my caring, confident, and ever-more-self-sufficient children. Kethlyn in particular was not having it. She was just finishing her freshman year at high school, and the last thing she wanted to do was start all over again in a different social group. So she put her foot down. She called in my previous promise, that I would not force her to move during high school.

And I didn't. I moved to California by myself, leaving my family in Texas, and I commuted home every weekend for three years. Most weeks, I would rush out of the office Thursday afternoon and tear down the highway at top speed, racing to get to the airport in time for the last flight to Dallas. Then it was a multihour plane ride, finally to arrive home when everyone was in bed. On Fridays, I worked from home, and all weekend I tried to spend as much time as possible with my kids. Maybe it wasn't the ideal situation for any one of us individually, but at the time it was the best choice for our family. Kethlyn was able to complete high school in the same school, and I was able to move forward toward my career goal.

30

Stay Flexible

Let me acknowledge for a moment exactly how much of my life had gone according to my grand plan, up until that point—from applying to only one university and getting in, to meeting Scotty right on time, to having my two healthy babies exactly when I wanted them, to Scotty finding his retirement opportunity, to successfully climbing the corporate ladder at IBM all the way to the executive plateau. Crossing each milestone required some combination of planning, research, creative problem-solving, preparation, smart choices, hard work, and yes, a fair amount of luck, both the kind of luck Scotty and I made happen and the kind that arrived like a gift. Now Silicon Valley was about to require yet another essential ingredient of success: flexibility.

Initially, I found it fairly easy to get recruited by California companies. Instead of ignoring calls from executive recruiters,

I started answering them, taking the opportunity to tell them what I was looking for in Silicon Valley. Now, this dynamic exists only in a hot, growing market where companies are struggling to hire key skills due to a dearth of experienced candidates. At this time, the web was new, it was booming, and there was a lot of demand for experienced leadership. I was prepared for opportunity to appear, and I was offered a position right away with a DSL provider, NorthPoint Communications. I thought this would be the perfect addition to my skill set. Already I had a strong technology and internet background; this would give me telecommunications. I believed the three areas were converging, and having experience across all three would help differentiate me.

Here's how badly NorthPoint wanted me: After several interviews, they called and offered me a job as head of sales. "You know," I said, "I've been listening to what you're trying to do, and yes, you need to streamline your sales. But you also need to better optimize your cost of sale, and you have other objectives that involve marketing. If you really want me to make a difference for you, I'm going to need to oversee your marketing as well." With that, I became executive vice president of sales and marketing, and I negotiated for NorthPoint to move my assistant's family to Silicon Valley as well. (For what it's worth, we did reduce the cost of sale by about 30 percent.)

I landed in Silicon Valley as the first dot-com bubble was on the rise. Gone was the corporate steadiness of IBM. Here, innovation, growth, and change happened at breakneck speed. In less than a year, after some ups and major downs, including filing for bankruptcy after a failed acquisition by Verizon, NorthPoint was bought out by AT&T. One of the NorthPoint board members introduced me to a company called Loudcloud, where I met Ben Horowitz. I joined as chief marketing officer in 2001 and soon became executive vice president of sales and marketing there as well. I was surfing at the top of the Silicon Valley wave.

And then it crashed.

Loudcloud had been helping tech businesses create, manage, and optimize their websites, but when the dot-com bubble burst, just months later, shuttering the doors of countless start-ups, our customer base was decimated. Loudcloud had hired me at a desperate time. They needed to lock down a whole new customer base as they pivoted to high-end enterprise services. It was all hands on deck, a complete repositioning and repackaging of the product, and we completely changed the direction of the company, moving away from targeting start-ups to targeting large enterprises. We had a heck of a team, and we pulled it off, in about nine months.

That was the good news.

The bad news was that Loudcloud had a capital-intensive business model, and raising cash was getting harder to do. Long story short, Loudcloud transitioned from a capital-heavy software hosting model that required a lot of cash investment to buy equipment ahead of earning revenues, to an asset-light software model that required relatively little cash investment up front. They sold the bulk of their business and revenue to Electronic Data Systems. The company was shrinking to a fraction of its original size. It was time for me to move forward.

Before I go on, let me say a little something about setting goals and taking risks. I had followed my CEO goal all the way to California, away from my family and as a sole breadwinner. In a hot job market, this felt like a calculated risk, a relatively secure one. After the dot-com bubble burst, I would need to double down and take greater risks, but—and this probably won't surprise you—*I had planned for this.*

First of all, I had my husband's full faith and support.

Second, we are savers. We had money in the bank—not a ton, but enough to live on if I found myself out of a job for a while.

Finally, I trusted in my abilities, reputation, and resilience. At this point in my career, I believed I could always get a job— maybe not *the* job I wanted, but at least a job that would pay the bills.

With this foundation in place, I felt confident enough to take greater risks.

So imagine this: It's 2002, I'm almost forty, I've learned a great deal from NorthPoint and Loudcloud, and I'm feeling ready for my chance to be a CEO. Well, guess what. So are hundreds of other people. Many of the start-up tech companies in Silicon Valley had gone out of business, and the streets were littered with CEOs trying to find new companies to helm. Having been in the area only a few years, and despite my success at Loudcloud, I was an unknown. Not only that, but when people looked at me, I didn't exactly fit the CEO profile. Still, after all these years, nobody was looking at a tall black woman from the East Coast.

The timing was horrible. But remember what my parents taught me: I don't deal in drama; I deal in accepting reality and controlling what I can. The road to success looks different for everyone—I already knew this. Everyone has a different path toward their goals, and no one's path is entirely smooth. We all experience ups and downs—some of us more than others.

We all come across roadblocks and major hazards—some of us more than others. But if you stick with it, if you keep moving forward, if you remain flexible and creative and dedicated, you will find your way.

I wasn't about to give up on my goal, so I had to be realistic, flexible, creative, and pragmatic. I did my homework. I talked to venture capitalists, entrepreneurs, and people who had been in Silicon Valley longer than I had. I determined that, with all the CEOs on the market who were better connected than I was, I wasn't going to find an opportunity at a top-tier company. Here's how it worked in that scene: Investors had their stakes in various companies, and they would connect their "best" CEO candidates with the companies they were pretty sure were going to be successful. I knew I wasn't going to get into those circles. But I also knew that if I could get into a company that wasn't a sure thing, I could turn it around. I didn't have to start in a great place—but I could get there. What I wanted was a company that needed fixing and that had a top-tier VC firm as an investor. That way, when it was time to find my next job, I'd have the credibility of having worked for a top-tier firm.

I found my opportunity in a place called Zaplet. This company was perfect for me, by which I mean it was very broken but well connected, with a lot of potential. Their lead investor was Kleiner Perkins Caufield & Byers, a top-tier venture firm also referred to as Kleiner Perkins. They were searching for a CEO. I thought maybe, just maybe, this was going to be my shot.

31

Stay Connected

Okay, you already know how I feel about the myth of work/life balance. I don't look for balance; I look for integration. I don't believe in making sacrifices; I believe in making choices. The reality of having a family as a young, ambitious professional is this: You aren't there sometimes, and you miss things. That said, family is deeply important to me. So I made every effort to show up in that place I love to be, with my people. But I also had to work on setting expectations. Especially once I moved to California, I had to think about how to show my kids how important they are to me, while still honoring my professional responsibilities. I came up with the idea to make agreements with my kids, and to strive never, ever to break a promise.

I learned a great strategy from Carol Bartz, when she was CEO of Autodesk. Carol and I had been introduced by a mutual friend. We met for coffee and learned we had quite a bit in common, including size 11 feet. In the course of that conversation, she shared with me an approach that made a huge difference in our family. Every time Kethlyn or Kheaton started a new activity or semester, we would take a look at all their games and recitals and so on, and I'd come up with an idea of how many I could probably attend. Then I'd make them a promise: "I will come to at least four of your games this semester." Then I'd try to show up to six games. That way, if I couldn't get there every time, at least I fulfilled my promise for the four games. If I made it to all six, we were all that much happier about it. I never once wanted my children to look out in the stands, searching for a mother who wasn't there.

I also had a firm promise on phone calls. I told my kids that if they ever wanted to talk to me, they just had to call. Even if it was in the middle of the workday, if I could take their call, I would. And if I didn't take the call, but it was really important, they had only to call a second time and I'd answer. This gave them the firm message that, even though my job got the bulk of my time, my children held the primary spot in my heart.

Of course, when I was commuting from Dallas to Silicon Valley for work, staying present with my family became a bit more challenging. One of the best connecting hacks came to me as a surprise from Kethlyn, who was a sophomore in high school during my first year in California. On that Mother's Day, when I opened Kethlyn's gift, I was a little confused. It was a thin book with travel symbols on the front of it. It looked like one of the blank books you see at the stationery store.

"Open it," Kethlyn said, so I did.

On the first page, I found this:

Dear Mom,

I bought this book so that we could stay better in touch. So I'll keep it one week and write down my thoughts, and then I'll give it to you. And you can take it the next week and you write down your thoughts.

Love, Kethlyn

As I read that note, I started to cry. After all the struggle, all our time apart, all the big changes I had put my daughter through—*she* wanted to be in closer touch with *me*. I was overwhelmed with gratitude for Kethlyn, that she cared so much and loved me through everything.

We did keep in touch, every week. In fact, I really enjoyed writing my thoughts in the journal and sharing them with her.

My apartment in California was a sparse, empty rental, the kind of place you might get when you're recently divorced. It felt odd and frankly a bit depressing to come home to that lifeless place. Although Scotty and I spoke every evening, and I talked to the kids frequently, I missed the physical environment of home. So I wrote in the journal about what had happened during my day.

Hi Doll,

I just finished another long day. We had a key channel partner in for meetings, trying to get them to increase their DSL line orders with us. And I had to finalize the board presentation for sales and marketing. Now I'm sitting in my barely furnished apartment, eating a salad and a heated frozen dinner, wishing I was home with you guys, enjoying your dad's cooking. The evenings are the worst. But this is the trade-off we are making so that both you and I can have what we want. As I stare at these blank white walls, I just have to keep reminding myself that I want to be a CEO and I want you to experience high school without moving. That's why I'm here in this empty apartment. Love you.

It wasn't much, just a diary, but it helped. Even more than recording my thoughts, I loved to read what Kethlyn wrote about her life. It made me feel like we were managing this pretty well, that my family was on a positive path.

Bottom line: If you choose to combine career and family, you will need to make trade-offs. But with creativity and cooperation, your family can find unique ways to stay connected, even when work takes you far from home.

32

Never Say Die

Before I committed to Zaplet, I needed to do my due diligence on both the company and the key investor. I asked In Sik Rhee, the CTO at Loudcloud, to investigate the software for me. He assured me Zaplet had a software foundation I could work with. Next, I started asking people about Vinod Khosla, the Kleiner Perkins partner responsible for the Zaplet investment. I learned he was really smart, worked hard for his companies, and had a record of success. I also learned he was strong willed and had a reputation for whipsawing companies.

As I headed to my first meeting with Vinod, I was pretty confident he was going to offer me the job. I'd already been negotiating compensation with the firm's human resources partner. But I had one crucial question left, and I suspected my asking it could change Vinod's mind about hiring me. Walking into his office, I felt nervous, excited, and determined all at the same time. Here he was, walking around his desk to shake my hand, gesturing toward a small table surrounded by chairs. I sat down, admiring the large photographs of his four children that filled the walls of his office.

After some small talk, Vinod updated me on the results of his due diligence of me; then he offered me the CEO job. I took a deep breath, looked him straight in the eye, and said, "Thank you, Vinod. I just have one question." I took another slow breath. "You have a great reputation for supporting your companies, but you also have a reputation of being strong willed and sometimes dominating. I just need to know before I answer, are you hiring me to implement your strategy for the company, or are you hiring me to be the CEO?" *Whew, I asked it!*

Vinod looked right back at me. A long, uncomfortable pause. Long enough for all kinds of self-doubts to run through my head. *Did I offend him? Did I blow it?*

Then his steely gaze softened a bit, and the corners of his mouth threatened a smile. "Shellye, I have strong opinions and a strong personality. Sometimes CEOs mistake this for being directive. I would be hiring you to be the CEO, to run the company, fully responsible and accountable."

Yes!

I'll never forget that day in December 2002. I walked out of Vinod Khosla's office, got into my car, and called my husband. "Scotty," I said, "I got the CEO job."

"Of course you did," he said.

A CEO by forty. I had reached my goal. Now it was time to get to work.

⌣

Prior to the dot-com bubble burst in 2001, Zaplet had been a hot start-up, raising over $100 million in venture capital. When I started in December of 2002, less than 10 percent of that money remained. Their software platform had been designed to help IT departments build apps quickly and easily. But after the bubble burst, IT departments weren't spending money on anything that didn't have an immediate return on investment, and Zaplet's software platform didn't. Sales to new customers had basically stopped. The company's cash expenses were greater than the cash they collected. My job was to turn this company around, fast, or it was going out of business.

It would be a race against the clock. I had to minimize the cash burn, to give myself time to develop a new strategy for the company before the money ran out. We cut costs where we could, and I began looking for business problems, not internally but externally. For the company to succeed, it had to help organizations solve problems that were causing them real, measurable pain. I needed to figure out which of these problems we could solve, leveraging Zaplet's software. I set out to speak with smart people who focus on market trends, interact with senior executives, and invest. I didn't ask these people for advice on building Zaplet; I asked them to tell me about the hard problems companies were struggling to solve.

Roger McNamee was the first person to mention the challenge of compliance with rules and regulations. In the earliest days of the internet, it was like the Wild West. There were no rules. But as the number of web-based business operations grew, so did new rules about what you could or couldn't do with people's personal data. Governments around the world were enacting more and more regulations for online businesses, and the fines and consequences for noncompliance were growing significantly. But compliance wasn't always easy for these companies, especially with the rules changing so quickly. I'd found our problem: We could leverage Zaplet's software platform to create applications that would help companies manage compliance, thus mitigating their risk exposure to the real costs of noncompliance.

We now had a strategy. But transforming the organization I had into the one I needed to execute on this strategy was going to take time and money, and I didn't have extra of either. Around this time, Vinod introduced me to Gunjan Sinha, the CEO of MetricStream, a smaller company focused on quality management and operational compliance. In the fall of 2003, we agreed to combine the two companies to target what we believed to be a new software category: comprehensive compliance and risk management. With the new strategy and combined company, we were able to raise investment dollars to fund our execution.

For the next couple of years, we built software applications and solutions for compliance management, risk management, internal audit, and such. In 2005, we launched ComplianceOnline.com, the first portal for compliance and risk professionals that provided content, training, and best practices to our target market, while providing us with insights and business leads. We pushed hard from 2005 through 2007, an unknown company trying to convince large enterprises that we could solve one of their thorniest problems. In early 2008, we caught a break. The industry analyst Gartner published a research paper, "Magic Quadrant for Enterprise Governance, Risk and Compliance Platforms," which described this new market and highlighted the market leaders. MetricStream was named a leader! Finally, our company was validated. Our phones started ringing with interest in and demand for our products. Our pipeline was growing. We needed to take advantage of the momentum, so we increased sales and marketing with the plan to raise new money for growth in 2009, on the heels of what we projected to be strong sales growth in 2008.

Well…that didn't go according to plan. Though we did increase sales, the stock market crashed on September 29, 2008. The Dow Jones Industrial Average fell 777.68 points in intraday trading, the largest point drop in history at that time. New sales came to a screeching halt, and suddenly MetricStream's bank balance was shrinking by the day. We had to cut costs and lay people off—a terrible turn of events for all of us. But the hardest decision was looming.

We entered January of 2009 with very little cash. Were we going to shut down the business or fight it out? To put the challenge in perspective, we had less than $2 million in the bank, and our quarterly payroll alone was more than that, not to mention the operational expenses we had to cover as well. It was time to strategize. We pulled MetricStream's top leaders together to map out a game plan. Everyone agreed: We were going to fight it out. We had come so far and had tasted the sweetness of success. We had worked hard for it, and we wanted that back. So we refused to die. As a matter of fact, we added "Never say die" to our culture motto. We worked and reworked the business model. The senior leaders agreed to pay cuts, and I knew what I needed to do.

Scotty knew MetricStream was in hard times, as so many companies were, so he wasn't completely shocked the evening I came home and asked him how he felt about me forgoing my salary for a year.

We had just finished cleaning up the kitchen after dinner, and he was perched on the kitchen stool. "Can we make it work?" he asked with an eyebrow cocked. "Have you run the numbers?"

I eased onto his lap. "I have, and we can. Our savings will take a real hit, but we can do it without any debt. Babe," I said as I cradled his head in both of my hands, "I know this wasn't the plan, but we have worked so hard to get MetricStream to this point. I know we are solving real issues, and I know governance, risk, and compliance will be a big opportunity. I believe in the team. If anyone can make this company succeed, we can. But it is high risk. We are in this together, Scotty. What do you say?"

He looked into my pleading eyes, smiled, and kissed me. "I've been poor before."

We laughed and hugged. After twenty-four years of marriage, I was ready to marry him all over again. And, with his support, I was ready to turn this company around. Again.

33

Keep Learning

Meanwhile, on the home front, as focused as I was on the three qualities Scotty and I wanted to teach our children, they were growing into their own, and I was becoming aware of the lifelong lessons they were teaching me.

Kethlyn graduated high school and chose to attend a historically black university. I wholeheartedly supported her choice, happy that she would be able to learn more about African American culture, just like her father, who also graduated from a historically black college. Like most teens do, she had weathered the bumps and bruises of the high school years. Despite our shared book during my commuting days, in hindsight I wonder if Kethlyn and I were as close as we could have been. I had started my CEO role in her senior year of high school. I had so much heavy lifting to do to fix Zaplet, the hours were crazy, and my mental capacity was being stretched. I did notice a bit of a dark cloud over Kethlyn at times—she'd get a little moody, yet swear nothing was wrong, and then she'd be fine a day later. But really, what teenager doesn't do that? I had faith that Kethlyn's self-sufficiency, confidence, and caring would take her wherever she wanted to go.

With my promise to Kethlyn fulfilled, after she graduated it was time for Scotty, Kheaton, and me to reunite. My Silicon Valley career was churning along, so they chose to leave Dallas and join me in California. Finally, I was going to have a stable home again—missing one important member, of course, but still, I was eager for the reunion. It would be nice to get a hug at the end of a stressful day.

Not long after we settled into our new home in California, we invited Gran to move in with us. She was living on her own at the age of eighty-eight, and her health was starting to fail for no good reason. I didn't want that for her—I wanted her with family, and especially with me. By now, Gran and Scotty were old compadres—she used to say she couldn't love him more if she'd given birth to him herself—and of course she loved her great-grandbaby, Kheaton, now a teenager. So she moved into the third bedroom of our four-bedroom home. I was ecstatic to have what felt like a real family dynamic again. For Kethlyn, this felt different. With Gran moved in, and the fourth bedroom reserved as a guest room, Kethlyn didn't have a room of her own in our new house. To me, this didn't seem like too big a deal, since she was all the way on the other side of the country, at Spelman College, and I was sure we would still make her feel like this was her home whenever she came to visit.

Scotty and I were both excited about this time in our lives. After many years as parents, we now had just a single teenager at home. We felt it was a good time to start thinking about who we wanted to be as adults in this new community. Just as my parents had done, we had always treated every move, except Japan, as if it would be long term. But on some level, I think we both saw Silicon Valley as a place where we might settle in for a while. So we started planning outings and parties, getting to know people.

One Saturday, after a couple of months in California, Kheaton came into the kitchen to grab some food. He was growing now, at fourteen, and always hungry.

"So, Dad," he asked, "what are we doing this weekend?"

Scotty raised an eyebrow. "Well, I don't know, what do you want to do?" He glanced at me, then back at Kheaton. "How about you, Bud? Got any plans?"

He didn't.

They figured out a plan, and I didn't think much about it until a few minutes later, when Kheaton retreated to his room to play video games.

Scotty put both hands on the counter. "Now what do you think that was about?" he asked me.

I was finishing up the dishes, so I hadn't been paying a lot of attention. "What was what about?" I asked, folding the dish towel over the rack.

"Have you noticed that everything we do, it's always the three of us?"

"You mean Kheaton? Well, we *are* the three of us, aren't we?"

"Shellye, don't you think it's odd that he hasn't made any friends of his own yet?"

That caught me. I stopped and put a hand on my hip. "Scotty, you know what, you're right. I haven't heard about a single friend yet."

Scotty's eyebrows pushed together. "So, if I think about it, didn't we discuss once that every time we moved to a new place, Kheaton's first friend was the brother of Kethlyn's first friend?"

"Oh my God, you're right. Scotty, he's never had to make friends without his sister before!"

Scotty laughed. "Well, he'll figure it out. I just hope he meets somebody he likes soon."

We never really knew what was going on in our son's mind at the time, but now he'd tell you that our serial relocations were a master class in social skills. For the first couple of months after we arrived in California, while Scotty and I worried, Kheaton was just learning how to fit into a new school without his big sister there to act as the wedge. In the end, it was his enthusiasm for extracurricular activities that served as his wedge, and when basketball season started, he made plenty of good friends.

Kheaton's approach was a big lesson for me. My life had been defined by ambition, moving forward, a resistance to waiting. Patience was not one of the well-used tools in my toolbox. To watch and wait with my son—to observe him watching and waiting—didn't come naturally for me. But I learned Kheaton needed to do things his way and on his time. Like me, he set his own schedule for moving through the world. But I wouldn't recognize that until years later, when the same kid who once had considered school unimportant graduated magna cum laude from Howard University.

While patience was my challenge with Kheaton, Kethlyn and I struggled with a different set of issues. Despite the efforts of our shared notebook, Kethlyn and I drifted apart during her latter teenage years. We just weren't communicating and sharing like we used to do. She seemed to be in control, in her own world, and didn't appear to need me. Reflecting on it now, I believe I was somewhat envious of the roles everyone else played in her life, because my role had taken a back seat. I'd worked hard to provide more comforts and experiences for her and her brother than I'd had growing up, and although that was fulfilling, I wanted to be more than just the provider. I wanted to be needed. Now she was growing apart from me, leaving me outside looking in. It was hard and painful.

I didn't know what was happening back then. I just knew that despite loving each other, we were broken. As I felt her slipping away, I wanted to hold her closer. This manifested itself in arguments over curfews and time spent with family versus friends. She would go spend the night with friends to avoid confrontations and dealing with our issues—but she was a teenager. How else did I expect her to handle it? On top of everything else, I wasn't home, so the emotional space between us was compounded by the actual physical space between us. It was so hard, and we carried all of this baggage as she went off to college.

I could probably count on two hands how many times we had deep conversations during her early college years. We both dealt with our fair share of personal growth during this period. Kethlyn navigated new environments, traumatic experiences, and new relationships without me, even though she wanted and needed me there. And I dove into work and kept trying to find the right way and the right time to cross the ocean between us. As with most things, there is no perfect timing, and there was no perfect moment for me to simply swoop in, so we took it one phone call at a time. As she got older, Kethlyn started to realize that I wasn't only her mom, I was also human, and she was my first child. I remember very clearly in one of our conversations I just stopped her and said, "Kethlyn, you're my first child. I have no idea what I'm doing. I'm operating without a net!" I could plan all parts of my life, but this one was going to require us to plan together to figure out how to get the relationship we both craved. So we did, day by day, phone call by phone call.

Fast forward to ten years after graduating from Spelman College, when Kethlyn was nominated to speak at the 2017 convocation. In an Instagram post, she made her pitch to the selection committee:

How do I manage to "be" in all of these roles (woman, employee, entrepreneur, mom, wife, and friend), and also be a successful, happy person? The answer: I made strategic decisions about all facets of my life: the jobs I took (and turned down), the type of person I would marry, how to plan our finances/schedule our lives so we could go after the things we dreamed about, and prioritizing my physical and mental health, especially after my children were born. I was purposeful and, frankly, unapologetic about setting a standard for what I needed and in putting myself first. That is why I want to encourage you to set your own strategy... unapologetically.

My heart burst when I read this post. Despite the ups and downs of our relationship over the years, my shortcomings,

188

and learning "on the job," she still became a confident woman. Kethlyn's post describes exactly what I'd hoped my daughter would understand about life: You always have a choice, and you have the right to make your choices and stand by them without guilt. This is true for you, too: You get to make your choices, and you get to follow through on them, unapologetically.

34

You Deserve It

In the end, Zaplet, the broken company entrusted to my care, became the little company that could. Over the next ten years, with a brilliant team and a terrific partner, Gunjan Sinha, we scraped together every bit of potential and molded it all into a vibrant, successful corporation now known as MetricStream. We earned our rankings on the Red Herring Top 100 and the Deloitte Technology Fast 50 lists. The software analysts named us as industry leaders every year. From the forty-five people we started with, we grew to employ over a thousand. We won awards, and we served customers all over the world. Yes, we faced near-death experiences several times during those years, but we acted on our rallying cry, "Never say die," and we thrived. I'm tremendously proud of what the team has accomplished.

I'm equally proud of all the ways my strategizing—for my own career goals, for my family, and for the company—led me to live my best life. I thank Shellye the sixteen-year-old for boldly setting the goal that guided me throughout my career, and Shellye the college student for envisioning the partner and family who would support me along the way. And, of course, I thank my husband, Scotty, and our children, Kethlyn and Kheaton, for accompanying me on the journey. Though in some ways my story reads like a fairy tale, there were no magic beans or fairy godmothers involved. It was all about ambition, foresight, planning, flexibility, and hard work. You know what that means? It means you can do it, too. No matter where you are starting or what your career and life goals, you can strategize your way to success. Believe in yourself. Set your goals. Go after them. Reap the rewards. You deserve it. These are the messages I want you to take with you.

There's an underlying belief in America that no matter who you are, if you just work hard enough, everything will work out for you. That's not true. It's more like, if you work strategically, you can improve the odds you'll succeed. I believe each of us is carrying a backpack. In that backpack are all the things you've been handed in this life. You don't get to control what's in your backpack. Sometimes, its weight is so onerous that no matter how hard you work, you always feel like you're struggling to keep up. Wearing that backpack all the time, you can get used to it. You may begin to believe you created that weight yourself, or that you deserve to be weighed down. That also isn't true. You deserve the freedom to set your life goals and walk toward them.

Everyone's backpack is different. For some of us, it's weighted down by inequality from the beginning; for others, it's the weight of tragedies that happen along the way. Some of us shoulder family or health problems; others get caught in economic or political disasters. For minorities and women of my generation, our backpacks have held more weight—greater household demands, the challenges of fitting into male-dominated workplaces, assumptions about our abilities, desires, and ambitions. In addition, we have lugged the weight of societal expectations about how we should look, dress, and speak; how we should keep our homes and care for our children; even what we should want from life. I can't say that weight has been lifted off the next generation's shoulders, but I hope it's at least a little lighter than what we carried.

Certainly, today's generation has more role models. When I was a young professional, I didn't see black women leading companies. Now we see Ursula Burns at Xerox, Oprah Winfrey, Rosalind Brewer at Starbucks, and Channing Dungey at ABC. We see African American women working as senators and serving on corporate boards as well. It remains a short list, but it has grown, and so have the lists of powerful people of all backgrounds and identities. Unquestionably, minorities and women are facing better odds than we were when I got started. Frankly, though, the odds still aren't great. For us, it isn't just a matter of "work hard, and you'll get what you want." It's more like, "If you know what you want, you can find a way to get it."

Yes, whatever's in your backpack is yours to carry, but—and I cannot stress this enough—it does not have to limit your goals. You can aim high, then strategize your way toward success. You deserve to live the life you want, on your terms. In the next section, I'll share my best advice for improving your odds.

PART FIVE

IMPROVING YOUR ODDS

35

Find Your Mentors

First, Sophia Velastegui bought me; then I almost broke her.

Sophia and I were both members of a professional women's organization called Watermark. I had offered up an hour of my time as part of a silent auction; Sophia was the winning bidder. She literally bought me—and paid a good amount of money for me. I was looking forward to hearing what she would have to say.

I didn't meet Sophia in person that day, but she contacted me soon after. Over the phone, I suggested we meet and walk, something I still do—combine exercise with conversation. What I didn't expect was that my walking partner would be eight months pregnant.

It was a hot day in Redwood Shores, and I was a little concerned when she showed up in walking shoes, with a belly like a watermelon.

"Are you sure you want to do this?" I asked.

"Oh yes," she said. "I'm fine, really."

I immediately saw something of myself in Sophia: strong willed, ambitious, willing to do whatever it took. But I was worried as we strolled along the sunbaked streets. At first she kept up with my admittedly long stride, but soon she was wobbling.

I was relieved when she conceded she'd rather sit in the shade.

"That's a great idea," I said. "I'm supposed to be here for you, not the other way around."

There's an interesting dynamic that develops between mentors and mentees. As a mentee, when you first meet someone whose brain you want to pick, you may not know much about their personality. Your instinct tells you to do whatever they suggest. But the point of mentorship isn't to serve someone more successful than yourself; it's to ask them to serve you, in their own way.

Sophia already had gone above and beyond just by showing up in sneakers. But she had also paid for my time out of her own pocket. Why then should she put herself in physical discomfort, just to get some advice?

"Please," I said, once we were settled at a cafe, "tell me what I can do for you."

Sophia was a Korean American engineer in her early thirties. She was doing well, and she wanted to switch from the semiconductor industry to consumer electronics. But she was about to have a baby and wanted to take some time off.

"How can I do this?" she asked. "Is it smart to change industries mid-career? How do I keep my career moving forward as a mother?"

Again, I was touched. It was instantly clear to me that Sophia had sought me out for specific pieces of knowledge that not too many people in Silicon Valley might have been able to give her.

"Those are great questions," I said. "I can tell you what worked for me and what I might do in your situation, but I can't say for sure that what worked for me would work for everybody. You're at a big decision point in your career. What's really important is that you create a strategy and stick to it."

Over the course of the hour, we figured out her best approach. We decided she needed to get to know the consumer electronics industry, identify a role for herself in it, and network her way into it by marketing herself almost as if she were marketing a product.

"Figure out what you have to offer," I told her, "and figure out what you want people to do for you. Just saying you want to get into consumer electronics is too broad. As you meet people, tell them exactly what they can help you with. Set a specific goal, and tell everyone what you need in order to reach it."

As for the baby, I had one major line of thought: "Sophia, you are going to need to put yourself first. When you came out here today to walk with me, you could have pushed yourself too hard. I might not have noticed. Then instead of sitting here drinking ice water, you might be in an ambulance."

I advised Sophia to budget in such a way that she could afford to take as much time off as she wanted with her baby. "Give yourself time to recover," I told her. "A baby takes nine months to grow, and it will take you time to bounce back, too." I told her about how difficult it had been for me to return to work within weeks of Kethlyn's birth. "You are not going to want to be back in the office," I said. "Take the time you want." My decision twenty years prior was made in a different time, when maternity leave had a higher price to pay for women. A short leave was part of my plan, but that doesn't mean it is what everyone should do. The key is to develop your own plan that works for your collective goals.

It's been about a decade since that day, and Sophia has done very well for herself. She went on to work for Apple, then to become the product head at Nest. She is now a general manager at Microsoft. She has been awarded multiple patents for her work, and she gives back to the engineering community through board service and other activities. And a few times a year, she and I make time for a dinner, a lunch, or—yes—a walk.

⌒

I've been taking advice from mentors since before I entered college—and acting as a mentor since I was in my late twenties. Without a doubt, mentoring is one of the very best ways to improve your career progress and opportunities. But here's the thing: Most people go about it all wrong.

In business, it's common to have very formal mentoring relationships, through networking or professional organizations, for example, or even within a corporation, as a higher-up grooms a younger employee. The perception is that this is how mentoring works best: as a formal relationship between near-strangers who meet now and then. That style of mentoring can be very helpful, but do I believe it's the best way to get and give guidance? Not at all.

My first "mentors" were those IBM managers I cold-called to

ask for advice on various job roles. I never asked them to formally mentor me; I simply asked their advice on specific topics and, if they seemed amenable to it, brought them some follow-up questions. In fact, here's my big secret: Throughout my career, I've rarely asked people to mentor me. I simply adopted them, treating them like a mentor without ever formally asking.

Think about it. You're a busy executive or high-level manager with a stressful job. A young employee comes to you with a request, "Will you mentor me?" What's the first thought that goes through your head? "Oh no!" Your face freezes; you lean back in your chair. Two words blare in your mind: TIME COMMITMENT.

In a moment like that, a prospective mentor is assessing not only their own commitment, but also the prospective mentee's. Is this person going to show up to meetings, leverage the advice you offer, and close the loop with you, letting you know how it worked out? It's disappointing to offer advice and then never hear from a person again, so some people hesitate to step into this role.

So forget that whole dynamic. My approach has always been to make people my mentors without a formal ask. Sounds tricky, doesn't it? Stick with me.

I got my first hint of this strategy way back at IBM, when I was a marketing manager. The company was putting a mentoring system in place specifically for high-potential women and minorities, and I was given the opportunity to choose a person to be my mentor. So I went about it the way you might expect. I requested Roland Harris, a branch manager whom I knew pretty well and admired. We had a good relationship, and I thought he'd be an excellent mentor.

Shortly afterward, I got a call from Roland, and he did not sound happy. He got right to the point. "You put me down to be your mentor?"

My heart sank. "Well, yeah. I thought you liked me…"

He sighed. "Shellye, you've already got me. You need to pick somebody else."

Oh. *Oh!* A light bulb went on. Why was I asking somebody to mentor me formally, when he was already willing to give me any advice and support I asked for? *Roland was already my mentor.*

The real value in formal mentorship relationships comes from reaching outside your circle. Find that person who's got the knowledge, experience, and connections to get you to the next level. I resubmitted my mentorship request, and I put down the name of somebody I didn't know.

But Roland's words stuck with me. "You've got me." *How many other people do I have access to, without thinking of them as mentors?* This was the catalyst for my strategy: Adopt as many mentors as possible. As I saw it, if one person giving me advice was good, two were better. The benefits weren't going to stop adding up. So I set out to get all the free advice I could find.

Here's how I adopted mentors throughout the rest of my career: I made it very simple for them.

First, if I found out about somebody who could give me advice, I would find a way to run into that person. Just a quick conversation in the hallway, or poking my head into their office, or the cliché of catching them in the elevator. I'd ask them only one question—something very simple, a yes-or-no. Something they could easily answer, I hoped. Then I'd thank them and go away.

Next, I'd try to apply their advice, and a little while later, I'd catch them again, in person or through email, to close the loop: "Hey, I just wanted to say thanks for the tip. I tried it, and here's how it worked. That was super helpful, thanks so much."

Well, now they're feeling pretty good. They were able to help, and it was easy for them—not much effort, and look at the results.

So then I'd ask another question—a follow-up on what to do next, or another way to approach it if their first tip didn't get the full result I was after: "Here's what happened as a result of your advice. Here's what I am thinking of doing next. What do you think?"

And so on. You can see where this is going. It worked consistently, in particular because I was a high performer who was rising through the ranks, and my chosen mentors would start to feel they had contributed to my success. Which, of course, they had.

I believe that almost all people truly want to help, in their hearts. If you make it easy for them, and you make sure they see results, they feel wonderful about it. Eventually, my adopted mentors felt so good they wanted to brag a little and tell others about how they were helping. They might even say, "Oh yeah, I've been mentoring Shellye." As for me, I was always thankful and respectful, and I made sure helping me was easy. That approach paid off time and time again.

In all my years of talking about the "adopting mentors" approach, I've only had a few people apply that strategy to me. One of those is Kris Bondi, a marketing executive I met in the late nineties. I had hired her as a consultant, and apparently she had done her homework on me. She later admitted that she'd heard me talk about my mentor-adoption strategy, and she had decided to use it. It was subtle, I have to say. She simply reached out for small things, ran ideas past me, and so on. From the perspective of the mentor, I will admit it worked flawlessly.

I don't have space in this book to list—much less tell stories about—all the people who made a positive impact on my life and career. But Ken Thornton bears mentioning, as he was one of the earliest. I worked for Ken temporarily while his executive assistant went on leave. Now, this was at IBM, where "executive assistants" were not on the administrative track, but on the leadership track. The job was offered to up-and-coming future executives as a chance to shadow executives, to learn their jobs, and to network. This was an incredible opportunity.

One of my responsibilities was to go to meetings in Ken's place in situations where he had two meetings at the same time, or he had another conflict. I'd sit in, take notes, and then summarize the meeting for him in a voice mail. I took this responsibility very seriously, and at the beginning, I'd leave him long messages that covered everything that had happened in the meeting.

After the first few days, Ken and I had a checkpoint. "You're doing great, Shellye," he told me. "I'm very pleased with your performance. But these voice mails. They're just too long. You know, I get a lot of voice mail, and I really need you to keep it concise. Just give me the key points, that's it."

Okay. So I had some feedback, and I was determined to use it. The voice mail system at IBM allowed me to record a voice mail, then review it before sending it. The next voice mail I left for Ken was twenty seconds long—and it took me about thirty minutes to record. I'd record it, play it back, make some adjustments, and rerecord over and over until I got it as short as possible.

Ken never knew what I went through to get those voice mails in shipshape, and I didn't need him to—this was simply what it took to apply his feedback. In turn, I learned an important lesson about how to talk to executives, particularly male ones: concisely and efficiently. Make your point first, and then share context and support for it. That lesson has served me countless times through my career. I also believe not doing this is one of the reasons women feel they aren't heard in male-dominated meetings. By the time they set the context, they've been tuned out before they make their point. I share this to illustrate to you that acting on good advice takes dedication and hard work on your part. People aren't going to hand out free tickets or golden keys, but you'll reap rewards when you put their ideas to work for you.

Yes, if you want to increase your odds of success, you should be looking for mentors. As you do so, keep a couple things in mind.

First, there's almost nothing you will try in your lifetime that somebody else hasn't already done. I mean that with the utmost respect: You may be innovating, but rarely are you doing something 100 percent new. If you want to move forward quickly in your career, seek out the people who can help you do a better job in the role you have and the people who can help you understand what your next steps might look like.

Second, be aware that what worked for somebody else might not work for you. Your environment might be different from your mentors', and times change fast. When I looked at all the CEOs in the world and saw how few of them were black women, I didn't assume that meant *I* couldn't be a CEO, but I *did* assume I would need to find a unique route to get there. Ultimately, getting advice is great, but you have to put it through the filter of your reality.

So, see who's available to you, figure out what you want to learn from them, go get that knowledge, and work to apply it in your own way. Then let those mentors know how much they have helped you.

36

Build Your Network

Research has shown time and time again that those who network do better in their careers.[17] My own networks have been a major part of my success strategy, beginning with my family. A caveat: My family is *tight.* I know not every family functions this way, but I grew up surrounded by siblings and cousins and aunts and grandparents. Every holiday was a get-together, and if you ever had a problem, you had somebody to call. That has stayed true throughout my life, and it's affected every relationship I have had—from my marriage to my kids to friends. I guess I learned to trust in others—to trust that we are not walking through the world alone, and that people generally have our best interests at heart.

Even if your family is not your primary source of support, you're not alone. Each of us has our own networks: through school, work, community groups, and of course online. Yet not all of us call on our communities for help when we need it. This confuses me. Trust me, if you're ambitious, if you're setting goals and going after them, there will be times when you'll be glad for a bit of help.

Though my family makes up the nucleus of my support network, I began growing that network through student organizations at the Wharton School, I continued at IBM, and I extended my understanding of networking back when I was president of Blockbuster.com. I was on a plane with Blockbuster's CMO, Jim Notarnicola, when he asked me a question that surprised me:

"Shellye, who do you use to bounce ideas off?"

I smiled and rattled off a list of names.

"No, no." He cut me off. "I don't mean people at Blockbuster. Who do you talk to outside the company?"

"Oh." I looked at him, slightly stupefied. "I'll be honest, I never thought to use people outside the company."

I was less than a year out of IBM at this time. IBM is a huge corporation, so in the past, whenever I had needed advice, I'd always been able to find a colleague to give me answers. But Blockbuster was a lot smaller, and here I was at the top level; the pool of people who could advise me was pretty limited.

"I've always had people outside the company as advisors," Jim said. He shared a few names from his own list: all well-respected people in their fields, but not people I had ever considered turning to for advice. "Listen, Shellye, this has made all the difference for me," Jim told me. "You need people you can trust, who will give you an outsider's perspective when you need it."

I took that to heart, and I started looking for outside mentors right away. When I left Blockbuster and moved to Silicon Valley, I met one of the greatest: Bill Campbell, who was a Silicon

Valley icon before he passed away. Bill had been the chairman of Intuit, an executive and board director for Apple, and CEO of Claris (among other roles). Lucky for me, he was on the board at Loudcloud when I became CMO. So, as I do, I adopted him to be my mentor. I never asked, just worked my normal strategy. But frankly, I think we both adopted each other. We met once a quarter or so, and in time, he helped me get my CEO job by introducing me to Vinod Khosla.

As a CEO, I decided to push things further, and I joined Watermark. This is an organization specifically for women who have made their mark in the Bay Area—CEOs and upper-level executives, for the most part. Walking into a room of senior executive women was both refreshing and inspiring. In my day-to-day operations, I didn't cross paths with many senior women in Silicon Valley. Yet here they were. Conversations uncovered our shared experiences and empathy for each other. The comradery was addictive. If you think about it, the odds of becoming a CEO are minuscule. For perspective, just add up all the people who might work at a corporation during a single CEO's tenure. Then think about the number of women who actually make it to the C-suite. Once you reach this level, it gets a little lonely. Just like Jim Notarnicola said, having peers to talk to made all the difference.

Once I became involved with leadership organizations, I didn't want to quit. I wound up serving on the board of Watermark for over a decade, and under the Watermark umbrella, I also organized a female CEO peer group of my own. I had missed having peers. I needed a group with whom I could "let my hair down" and who could turn to each other for support. This CEO group was the one I consulted when I needed to change the capital structure of Zaplet. I had never done that before, and I didn't want to go to my board of directors for help; they were my bosses. They were also the ones who celebrated the closure of that key merger.

Once a joiner, always a joiner, I suppose. My involvement with organizations didn't end there. I also joined the C200 group (also known as the Committee of 200), an invitation-only group for women who are running businesses of scale. I got involved with the Information Technology Senior Management Forum, specifically dedicated to building the pipeline of African American executives in IT. And I joined the Silicon Valley Leadership Group, a public policy organization focused on improving economic health and quality of life in Silicon Valley. These aren't all the groups I've been a part of in my life—for example, I was on the board at Girls Inc. all the way back in Dallas—but these Silicon Valley organizations have been a special experience for me, probably due to my being a CEO when I joined. Not only was I in a position to develop relationships and gain contacts, I also had more power to help and give back to others.

Which brings me to my next point: You need to be building your network all the time, not just when you want something. In fact, aim for most of your interactions to be spent providing help or value to others. Give more than you take; it's not just the generous thing to do, but it also puts you in a position of power instead of weakness. This is especially important for people who may see themselves as marginalized or lacking opportunities and privilege. Establish yourself in the terms of what you have to offer rather than on what you might need. Doing so will affect your own sense of self-worth just as much as it affects the impression you make on others.

Speaking of making impressions—today, most people do their networking online. But as you build your networks, I encourage you not to overlook the importance of in-person connections. Meeting someone face-to-face is an entirely different and a much more memorable experience. This isn't to say you can't build powerful connections online, but there's something about spending time with a person in all three dimensions at once that more solidly cements the relationship. Keep that practice alive. Find the professional organizations in your area and go to their meetings, attend their conferences if possible, show up at their social events. As more people resort to digital communication, your ability to socialize in person may become an advantage. Not to mention, these professional organizations are great places to meet the advisors you need to talk to and to offer the value you have to share.

As a young girl, even with my close family ties, there were many times when I felt alone on my ambitious path. As I grew up, my personal and professional communities became huge parts of my life, reminding me that even when I'm "the only one in the room," I am not alone. Now I have access to nation-wide networks of peers and friends, including some incredible women and minority leaders. These groups have empowered and inspired me too many times to count. Even better, they have given me opportunities to mentor young professionals. I'm ecstatic to see the young, talented, diverse generation coming up through the ranks. I want the same for you.

You don't need to be alone on your path. Start building your networks. Offer what you can, and ask people to help you. The right ones will be happy you did.

37

Find the Current

Shellye, how did you do it? How did you get where you are today?" I've lost count of the number of times I've been asked this question. If I had to boil my answer down to one sentence, it would be this: I found the current, and I jumped in it.

I've said before that institutions are organized power. In order to rise through the ranks of a company, an organization, or even an industry, you need to understand how the power flows through it. So, at sixteen years old, when I decided I wanted to become a CEO, and I asked, "How do I do that?" what I was really doing was looking for the current. How does the power flow to that position I want to hold someday?

Of course, I wasn't thinking in terms of institutional power at that age. But understanding power dynamics was an ability I had developed as a young child, as a matter of survival. When you're the only black girl dropped into an all-white classroom during a racially charged time, you quickly learn how to read a room. Instinctively I knew I couldn't trust everybody. I knew everything wasn't just as it appeared. To protect myself, I became a keen observer. I watched people to figure out what was really happening, not just what people said was happening. Initially, that was how I protected myself, but that skill also became a means of propelling myself toward my goals.

When I set my sights on becoming CEO of IBM, I looked for the current running through the corporation, and I identified the tributary most likely to flow to the C-suite: Sales. This first step out of college didn't make sense to many of my peers, because it lacked the prestige expected of a Wharton graduate. But by my assessment, it made all the sense in the world: At IBM, the people who had earned the position I wanted had started in sales. I'm not saying that was the only way to get where I wanted to go, but when you're ambitious and you want to move quickly, you need to jump in the current that's already moving. So I jumped into sales.

By the way, let me take a moment here to make a pitch for starting out in sales. To this day, I tell people I don't care what you want to do in life, the best first job is a sales job. Best job. Why? In sales you learn to ask for what you want and need. You learn to be resilient. You learn that a no is not the end of the world; it just means "not now." You learn how to negotiate. You learn how to listen. You learn to develop relationships. In fact, the act of selling is the act of finding the current. When you enter a room to make a pitch, you read the room to find the power, noticing whom people defer to, identifying the decision makers, understanding where you need to focus your attention, watching body language to know when you've engaged people's attention and when you've lost them, adjusting to flow with the current. You learn to assess people's problems and to become the person who can solve them. All of these qualities and skills will serve you well as you progress through your career.

Anyway, back to IBM. I followed that current to some un-expected places—like Japan—and when it became clear it wouldn't lead me to the CEO position, I began looking for another current. At that time, the power was flowing toward the internet, and after a brief stop in Dallas, I followed it to Silicon Valley. Just as a river is going to find its way around a rock, when my flow was blocked, I found my way around the obstacle When the dot-com bubble burst and I suspected I wouldn't find an inlet into a CEO position at an A-play company, I went a different way. I found the current that worked for me.

Ultimately, when it comes to reaching your goals, the real skill lies in spotting the strongest current—in an organization, in an industry, even in the larger economy—and then positioning yourself so it propels you forward. Sail past the opportunities that will lead you into the weeds, and take the opportunities that will move you toward your goals.

38

Take Risks

There are no two ways about it: **Vulnerability is an un-avoidable side effect of ambition.** Pursuing your career and life goals involves taking risks. When you ask a mentor for advice, you make yourself vulnerable. Same happens when you try something new, when you go after something you really want, even when you fall in love—you open yourself up to risk. **If you avoid taking risks, you limit your opportunities.** But in the process of taking a chance, you can transform your risks into rewards. Risk and reward: two sides of the same coin. So how do you develop the confidence to flip that coin?

As you've read, I've taken some pretty risky leaps in my career. When I look at the ecosystem that made this risk-taking possible, I see a few essential elements.

First, **I have support, both at home and professionally.** With Scotty as my number one cheerleader, and the rest of my family surrounding me, when I stepped into new situations, I knew I would have the emotional support I needed. Further, because I had built a network of mentors and peers, I knew I'd have a number of advisors to turn to if and when I needed help. Also, I knew I would *ask* for the support when I needed it. (What good is a support network if you're not going to take the risk of asking for help?)

Second, **I developed a trust in my own abilities**. The more risks you take, the more familiar you become with the process. As you build a track record of reaping the rewards, you develop confidence in your skills and judgment. Even if you rack up a fair share of mistakes, you're developing resilience—learning the lessons and moving forward. Sure, when I take risks, I know I might fall, but I also know I'm not going to fall *that* far. Not only have I built an ecosystem that supports risk-taking, but I have fallen before, and I can trust I'll be able to get up again.

Third, **I look at fear versus fact**. When people ask me if I'm nervous about a risk I'm taking, I'll say "Sure, I have concerns, but I mitigate my fear with facts." Before making a decision, I learn as much as I can about my new opportunity, and then I place these facts side by side with my fears. I ask, "What is the real value of this opportunity? What are the potential rewards?" Then I ask, "What's the worst thing that could happen?" Once I've identified my worst-case scenarios, I ask myself, "Can I live with that?" If the answer is yes, I take the risk. I know a number of people who have turned down opportunities, offering some plausible rationale, but in many cases I suspect it was really fear that caused them to back away. I can't help but wonder what could have happened if they had learned to mitigate their fear with facts.

Finally, **when we hear about risks other people have taken, it becomes easier to think about taking our own.** So for the sake of inspiration, let me share some stories with you.

~

In the mid-2000s, I heard from a man named Kevin Clark, an African American Wharton graduate who had worked for my organization at IBM. Kevin and I have spoken on and off over the years, in a loose mentorship relationship. This time, he called me because he was in trouble and he needed advice. His work environment had become toxic, and he was considering walking away from his job; but he'd been there less than two years, and he was worried about how that was going to look when he was applying for new positions.

"Kevin, from what you've told me, your problem isn't with one person. It's the culture," I said. "This company culture isn't one you want to work in, and as an employee, you get to choose what to do about that."

He cleared his throat. "Uh, so what would you choose?"

"Okay, so normally I tell people not to leave a job before they have another one lined up. But, Kevin, I think you need to leave now, before it gets worse. These things have a way of taking people down with the ship."

"Okay." Then Kevin asked, "So you don't think there's some way I can fix things here?"

"I think you need to focus on changing the things you can control, versus those you can't. From your story, I'm hearing that your bosses have already showed you they aren't interested in your attempts to make things better. So what *is* in your power to change?"

Knowing it was a huge risk for Kevin to jump without a safety net, I coached him to take the leap. He had told me that he and his wife had savings. I knew he was smart, capable, and motivated, and **I knew he was going to gain more from taking that risk—from making himself vulnerable—than he would from staying in a dangerously unhealthy situation.** Kevin took my advice. It was scary, and it did take him a little while to find a new job, but once he did, he accelerated rapidly in his career. Now he's running consumer marketing operations for Facebook. The risk freed him up mentally and professionally to accomplish greater things, on his own terms.

Just before he started at Facebook in 2017, Kevin called me again. This was a big move for him, and now, as a fortyish adult, he wanted to talk about how to work with Facebook's younger, tech-elite employees. "I need to present some key initiatives to the entire team in my first week," he said. "I want to make the right first impression, and I want to impress my bosses, too. What would you do?"

I smiled. This reminded me so much of my first presentation in Japan—walking into a room full of people with a different cultural background, wanting to address their needs, make a positive impression, and establish good relationships with them. "You need a message that will resonate with them. You know, *purpose* is key to millennials. Don't just talk about the initiatives, talk about why they're important," I explained. "I would go in with the servant approach. **Don't think about how to make yourself look good; think about how to make everyone's job easier. Work with people by helping them. Make it so that, after thirty days, they're wondering how they ever managed without you.**"

That's exactly what Kevin did, and I was glad to hear it worked for him. That piece of advice was one I'd received years before, from an executive named Curt Gadsden. Curt adopted me when I got my first full-time executive assistant job, working for David Thomas, who ran North America for IBM. I was just one step away from the executive level, and Curt, who was also African American, took special interest in me as a minority female on the executive track. He set up a meeting to explain that he wanted me to succeed.

"You're an EA now," he said, "and that means your job is to make your boss look good. Other EAs are trying to make themselves look good, but if you want to really excel, you're going to make him wonder how he could ever do his job without you."

Got it. I knew how to do that. But Curt had more to offer.

"And then," he continued, "I want you to think about how you can be a good partner to all the people who report directly to your boss. Think about it: It's very likely that your next job will be working for one of them. They keep an eye on everyone at your level, and when it's time to make a hire, they're looking for somebody who is indispensable, a valuable team player."

That was a big light-bulb moment for me, and I've tried to keep the servant mindset in every job since. It has always paid off. In fact, Robin Sternbergh, who hired me for my first executive job, did indeed work for David Thomas. Now that advice was helping Kevin, too.

⌒

Not long before writing this book, I had lunch with a female executive who shared with me that she was considering leaving her current company over the gap in pay between herself and her male colleagues.

"Do they know you want to be paid more?" I asked. I was thinking about my own experience years ago at IBM, with the skip-level manager who didn't know I was willing to move to get a promotion.

"Of course they know," she said. "I bring it up every year at my review."

"But what about the rest of the year?"

"Well, no. It doesn't really come up."

"Listen, you need to ask for what you're worth," I told her. "At the end-of-year review, every single person they talk to is asking for more money. It's a standard request, and they are not likely to understand how important that is to you. You've got to bring it to their attention. Let me ask you: If you were paid better, would you want to stay?"

"Yes, I think I would," she said.

"Then don't quit; try to talk to them again about pay."

This advice rings all too true for so many of us whose backpacks are a little heavier. **After a lifetime of being asked to demonstrate our worth and play by strict rules in order to succeed, we begin to believe that being passed over is a sign that our skills and abilities aren't valued. Sometimes that is true, and you may need to look for opportunities elsewhere. But sometimes you're not getting what you want because you haven't asked the right person yet.** How will you know, if you don't ask? Sharing your dreams and goals isn't easy. It can make you vulnerable to comments and criticism. But sometimes you have to be audacious and just go for it. At least then you will know what's available for you, so you can plan your next steps.

⌒

Speaking of audacious, several years ago, my goddaughter Crystal shared with me her career plan: She wanted to have her own day care business. She had already worked as a teacher, and she had earned her MBA. So I advised her to go get a job at an existing day care to learn how the business runs. Off she went to apply for jobs. But a few months later, she still hadn't been hired.

"What's the problem?" I asked.

"Well, I thought because I've been a teacher already, I didn't want to go for a teaching job; I wanted to be hired as an assistant director. But I haven't been getting any calls. Do you think I should go back to being a teacher? Would that help me get hired?"

"I don't think so. It seems to me like you're ready for at least an assistant director job," I said.

"Well...what if I apply to be a director instead?"

Not long after, Crystal landed a director job, and I was so proud. Turns out, with teaching experience and a master's degree, people thought she was overqualified for an assistant director role.

This is a significant difference I've observed between women and men: Most women won't go after a job unless they're sure they have all the requisite knowledge, skills, and experience; men will go ahead and try anyway. So, to see my goddaughter take her rejections and, instead of believing she was under-qualified and stepping down a level, test the waters at a higher level—well, it was affirming and inspiring. **It may feel risky, but it's perfectly acceptable to bring your core skills and relevant experience to the table, and then learn the rest on the job.**

Sara Madsen Miller was a friend of an old friend who introduced us purely because she thought I could offer Sara some advice. We met once for coffee, and since then, over the years, she occasionally gets in touch with specific questions.

Sara is focused on building her award-winning creative production company, and she asked me about growing her influence outside her home turf of Dallas. She wanted to be better known, to get connected regionally and nationally, and to sit on the board of a corporation or two.

"So how can I accomplish all that, if I have never done any of it before?" she asked. "How do you grow your reputation in a sphere where you have no reputation?"

"This is a tough one," I said. "You need to raise your profile, so people see you not at the level you're at now, but at the level you want to be."

I advised Sara to think aspirationally—to fake it 'til she makes it and take calculated risks. First, she developed her LinkedIn profile to focus on her work outside of Dallas; then she started publishing and got some press coverage in the region. Finally, I told her to keep scaling her own business, so she could show her results to companies seeking board members. As a result, she's now a board member for the Cotton Bowl Classic, and she is working on her next board seat.

And why not? **More often than not, risk precedes success— the boldness of saying what you want, the vulnerability of asking for what you need to get there, and the audacity to push in when you have a chance.**

What's the worst thing that could happen if you try?

Can you live with that?

Let me add one more question here: **Can you live with the consequences of not taking the risk? I see this too often—people staying in untenable situations because they are afraid to leave. Women and minorities in particular can face a lot of bias and discrimination in the workforce, but we don't have to accept it. We can make calculated risks to move past it.**

Recently my son-in-law told me about a woman he knew who worked in government. She knew she was being paid 50 percent less than her male peers working in the same job. When she confronted her boss, he told her, "You're a woman and your kids are of age, so I think you're being paid fairly." While that story aggravated me, it didn't surprise me much. What did surprise me was this woman's response: She didn't leave. She stayed in that job. And she's not alone. In March 2019, the *Financial Times* reported that UBS, a Swiss lending company, has a history of punishing women who take maternity leave: "More than a dozen women in the Swiss wealth management unit have complained about the treatment they received when they took time off to have children, which in many cases resulted in their bonuses being cut 30 percent or more." Again, this type of news is not terribly surprising, but this part is: The women have stayed. Why is that?

If your goal is to join forces with your colleagues and agitate for change, perhaps that's a reason to stay. **But if fear is keeping you locked in an unfair dynamic or unhealthy workplace, I urge you to consider what it might mean to make a change.** Remember? Risk and reward: same coin.

I don't say this lightly. I know what it feels like to realize discrimination and bias are blocking your progress, your opportunities, and your earning potential. By the time I recognized the writing on the wall at IBM, I had spent my entire career there since high school—head down, charging forward, determined to serve the company well and earn my way toward the C-suite. When my progress was blocked, I asked that scary question, "Am I really going to leave?" I understood how IBM worked—how people got promoted, how positions got made. I had developed my professional reputation there. My whole network was based there. So many of my friendships were based there. Leaving the mother ship would be a big deal. But the limitations were clear: I would not reach my professional goals at IBM. I felt like the fledgling bird getting nudged out of the nest by Mama. I knew I was going to have to leave, so I prepared to jump.

Once I accepted that I was leaving IBM, the question became "Where am I going to go?" I needed to find the next right job to lead me toward my career goal. And I needed to support my family while making the transition, because I was our sole bread-winner. I felt the weight of that for sure, but I also felt excited to explore the opportunities out there. And that's what I want you to remember: You are capable, you are talented, you are skilled, and you deserve every chance to succeed. **If something stands in the way of your rightful compensation or opportunities, I encourage you to take a risk and fly to the next big thing.**

39

Life Planning 101

You are going to live forever.

Well, maybe not for*ever*, but if you're in your twenties now and you lead a healthy and purposeful life, you will probably live another seventy to ninety years.[18] From *right now*. No longer does the average American professional have just twenty-five or thirty years to make a mark on the world. You may have a fifty-plus-year career, or even a seventy-year marriage. Just imagine that for a minute.

In other words—and I'm very happy to tell you this—you really don't need to figure out your whole life right away. You've got more time to try things, to make mistakes, to learn. Nor do you need to create a life plan that's quite as aggressive as the one I laid out for myself as a teenager. I am happy I married and had kids young—that worked for me. I'm glad I gave myself a head start on my career—that was my passion. But you've got your own passions and goals; you're on your own schedule. Honor that. All you need to do now is pick a direction—something you want to aim for—and start moving toward it.

Even if meticulous planning isn't in your nature, I want you to try something for me, a little Life Planning 101 for the unapologetically ambitious. This chapter contains a condensed version of my best advice for creating a life plan, starting from around the time you graduate college. It's the crib notes for the book, and I hope you'll get a lifetime of use out of it.

So indulge me, and let's get strategic.

LIFE PLANNING: THE BIG PICTURE

Whether you're choosing your course of study in college, about to graduate, or wanting to create a change in direction, there are five major areas where you may want to do some advance planning. Which areas you focus on are up to you; you can select only the ones that apply, or plan for all five. They are:

- Getting your first job
- Marriage or partnership
- Career planning
- Having children
- Long-term life plans.

Pick your categories and get ready to customize your plan.

GETTING YOUR FIRST JOB

Let's begin with your first leap into the workforce. Where do you want to land? How do you get there?

Which job?

When it comes to finding that first serious job, find an **industry**, a **role** or **discipline**, a **location**, and a **company** that will work for your objectives.

As you consider the **industry** to go into, look for growth. A growing field will have more jobs, more opportunities, and more chances for you to advance. Conversely, a shrinking or stagnant industry will be harder to get into, harder to stay employed in, and much harder to advance in.

Side note: This is where that non-advice, "follow your dreams," becomes problematic. Many of us have dreams of making beautiful art or music, for example. But finding work, much less advancing in those industries, can be very challenging. If you do choose to follow this direction, to support yourself you'll likely need to perform in the top 10 percent of your chosen field. Or you can find a job in a growth industry, where high-paying jobs are more readily available, and pursue your passions in your free time.

If you don't care too much about the industry you go into, consider the **role** you would like to play. Let's say you want to work in marketing. If you go into consumer packaged goods, for example, you will find more marketing jobs because that's a major part of the business. The financial services industry has marketing people, but it's not a core role. Choose an industry where you'll have a core role, as opposed to playing a supporting part. If you're not sure what role you want to play, this is a good time to reach out to people who have jobs that sound interesting and ask them what the work is like, what their industry is like, and what advice they might have for you. This can help you identify the roles that sound most promising to you.

Location can be a big factor for some people; for others, it hardly matters. Does it matter to you? If yes, think about industries and roles through a geographic lens as well. What industries have longevity in your target area, and what roles are most ripe for growth? If you live and want to stay in Wyoming, for example, you probably won't angle for a career in pharmaceuticals. Instead, you could look into mining or real estate.

If location doesn't matter, then you have to consider your willingness to relocate: where, when, and how often. If you choose to work for a large national or multinational corporation, then you may be looking at a lifetime of moves. Are you location-flexible? Or would you rather move to an area—such as Silicon Valley for technology, New York City for finance, or Houston for oil and gas—where you will have plenty of opportunities to advance in an industry without frequent relocations?

Once you've made your decisions on industry, role, and location, it becomes easier to identify the **companies** you might want to work for. Screen each company and find the ones that match your values. From a culture standpoint, where do you see yourself fitting in and learning? That's where you want to target your job search.

How to get the job

This could be a book in itself, but here are the broad strokes: **Use your available networks**, **search job listings**, and **volunteer**.

Whether you realize it or not, you have a network and access to others' networks. A network simply comprises people you know. These can be neighbors, friends, relatives, people who attend where you worship, or people with whom you play sports or engage in hobbies. Your network is made up of your friends and relatives as well. In addition, you can ask people in your network if they have people in their network who can help you. That is how you can access their networks.

To **use your available networks**, figure out if anyone in your network knows anyone in the companies you're interested in. If you are a recent graduate, your network will naturally center around your college. Speak to professors, advisors, and alumni with whom you have developed relationships. Take advantage of your school's career center. Then look at your other major networks: your family and friends. Talk to your relatives; do they have anyone in their networks who can help? How about your friends? And your friends' parents? Even if you haven't thought much about building a network, you have one anyway. Now let everybody know what you want to do and how they can help.

When you speak to someone in your network, ask if they have any advice or know anyone in your target industry, role, or company. This question in particular is key, and it's one that has served me throughout my career: **"Do you know anyone it would be helpful for me to talk to?"** By asking that question, you are leveraging not just your own network, but your contact's network as well. Most people want to be helpful, and especially want to be seen as well connected. So when you ask, they'll really think about it. Odds are good you'll be introduced to yet another person. And then you repeat the process.

Your next step is to **search job listings** for available opportunities. Now, typically, just applying for jobs you find online isn't going to bring you significant results. Instead, use the job boards to identify the opportunities you want, then leverage your network to gain an introduction or recommendation, so your résumé gets to the top of the pile.

Finally, you can **volunteer** until the right opportunities become available. Volunteering in the space where you want to build a career gives you experience and connections, which will eventually be your tools to acquire the job you want. Of course, you may not be able to volunteer directly for the company you want to work with; but you can work in that space. For example, if you want to be a marketing person in the pharmaceutical industry, you probably won't find entry-level volunteer positions in any corporate marketing departments; but you *can* find marketing opportunities elsewhere, like with a nonprofit. There you can build experience and a portfolio, so you'll have something to show prospective employers.

Now, I realize that very few people can afford to volunteer full-time. So if you are unable to find the ideal job, then take a job as close as possible to the role, industry, or geography you desire. Use the first job as a stepping-stone, and try to volunteer on the side. Typically, it is easier to find a job when you already have one.

How to succeed in your first job

Now that you've got the job, you want to do it well. Remember, no matter how ambitious you are, you'll advance in your career more quickly if you focus on the job you have and gain a reputation for good work. So **develop your performance**, **work on your reputation**, and above all, **do your homework** for how to succeed in your current position.

In fact, **doing your homework** is your first goal. Figure out how to make your boss's job easier. When you go in with a servant mindset—finding out how to support your team and your boss—after a few months they won't know how they ever managed without you. Next, talk to people who have done the job before you. Remember, no matter what job you're doing, it's almost certain that someone has done it or something similar before. So find those people, and ask for advice on how to do your job well.

Developing your performance will help you in this job, and it'll give you skills you can carry with you into future positions. Create 30-day, 90-day, and 180-day plans for yourself, with measurable goals. Ask your boss about the specific goals and metrics you are expected to reach, and always strive to meet or exceed them. Remember, the better you do in the job you have, the more opportunities you'll get to advance.

Finally, **work on your reputation**. It's one of your greatest assets. It starts with strong performance and sharing your successes in an effective way. People won't know what you've done unless you tell them. I'll give you an example: As CEO, I like to check in casually with my employees whenever I'm walking through their work areas. Just a casual hello, how are you. Some employees will say hi and tell me about their day, their activities, even their problems. But a handful of people stand out, because they give me a quick report on their recent accomplishments. "Doing great, Shellye. We just resolved a challenging issue at customer XYZ!" That's memorable, it takes next to no time, and it gives me a positive feeling about that person's dedication. You are your own best advocate, so advocate for yourself and your team.

In addition to sharing your successes, it's important to be a team player. Learn about the people you work with—their strengths and weaknesses, likes and dislikes. How can you create good team dynamics? Even if you're not managing a single person, you can still learn the working styles of the people around you and try to help leverage the right people for the right tasks, so you meet your objectives as a team. This is a skill you'll develop now and continue to use throughout your career.

MARRIAGE OR PARTNERSHIP

Though marriage and partnership have changed over time, I do believe the majority of people still hope to spend their lives in a partnership with another person. If this is a potential goal for you, I recommend you think carefully about the sort of person you'd want to commit to.

Understand "the package" that will work for you

This, too, could be an entire book, but for our purposes here, let me tell you this: When you're thinking about the kind of person you would like to commit to, you've got to start by knowing yourself. Every single one of us comes as a package: strengths, weaknesses, emotions, personality, baggage. We are who we are. What is the package you're working with already? What sort of partner can complement you?

Think first about **complementary characteristics**, the things you'd like to have in common with your partner. Scotty and I, for example, both like people. We like being social and being part of our neighborhood and community. What are some of the things you like about yourself and would like to share with a partner? What sorts of experiences and activities would you like to share?

Then think about **supporting characteristics**. These are the areas where you might need a little help now and then. For example, despite how confident I might appear, impostor syndrome has been a constant force in my life, especially in my younger years. I practiced "fake it 'til you make it" for a long time. So I knew that I wanted my life partner to be someone who was going to be my cheerleader, to tell me I was doing well in moments of self-doubt, to help me celebrate successes. What are the areas of your own life where you could use a little outside help?

This speaks to **personality** as well. For example, if you're introverted, would you like to be with someone who brings you out of your shell? Or would you rather find a partner who gives you space? The right partner for you doesn't need to be someone who challenges every one of your unique qualities. Some parts of your personality are integral to who you are, and the right partner will be comfortable with that.

You may have preferences about your partner's **skills** as well.

For me, I was not going to marry somebody who couldn't cook and clean, because I didn't want to do it all myself. You might want a partner who can fix things around the house, or balance a budget, or has any number of other skills.

Last but definitely not least, consider your **alignment on future plans**. What do you see your life looking like in the far-off future? If you're considering committing to a single person for many years, you probably want to share a similar vision of the future. Many couples break up during major life changes: shortly after having kids, when the kids go off to college, or at retirement. Why? I believe it's because they reach a fork in the road and have different ideas on which way they're going. It can be a heartbreaking disappointment. You will walk a long path with your partner; make sure you agree on which direction you're headed.

Finally, looking at all these pieces of the package, think about prioritizing them. Which of these areas are most important to you? It's not likely that you will find the ideal partner who fulfills every dream characteristic. So which do you really want the most? Also, consider what you can live with, because nobody is perfect.

Get aligned on how your relationship will work

What are your expectations for the life you'll lead? Does your partner share those expectations? What do you want out of life, and what conversations do you need to have in order to make that happen? A big one for me was the expectation that Scotty would stay home with the kids. It was important to me, and I made sure it was on the table before we decided to get married. What are your expectations? And I'm not just talking about the big ones. It gets more granular than that.

I believe it's very important to talk about the essentials of how your relationship will work. Remember, life is an accumulation of little moments, day to day. Think about how you want your home life to work. For example, **basic chores**. Who's doing the laundry? Who's cooking dinner? Who pays the bills, and who cleans the house? It's basic stuff, but it's important to talk about it before you embark on a life with somebody who may have very different expectations from yours. If you've ever argued with anyone over who should do the dishes, have this talk with your partner.

Of course, you should talk about **money**. Relationship dynamics around money are certainly shifting, and that means you really can't assume anything about how your finances will work. You may share accounts or not; you may budget for expenses in proportion to your relative earnings, or you may each "own" certain expenses. Get on the same page.

In addition, I believe it's important to discuss **career decisioning**—not just what your individual career aspirations are, and not just your plans, but also how you'll make decisions about your careers when those decisions impact your life together. For example, my career path involved a lot of moving around, and at a certain point, Scotty and I began prioritizing my job over his. We had discussed these moments—even planned for them—long before we reached any decision points, so we were ready to make the transitions when the time came.

Just like career and finances, a couple's expectations about **family commitments** can vary wildly. This can create a lot of stress on a relationship. Think about it: Where are you going to spend the holidays? What do you do when a family member needs financial help or caretaking? In my life, family has always been a big presence, including extended family. That means a lot of visits, and a lot of situations in which I'm expected to (and I want to) show up. Other families are smaller, more nuclear, or more distant. Discuss how you want to participate in your own and each other's families. Figure out what works for both of you.

Finally, of course, you're going to talk about **having kids**. Do you and your partner want them? When? How many? Certainly, most people have thoughts about children before they enter a relationship, yet too many couples break up after five or ten years because of a disagreement over having kids, or because they had different visions for what life would be like with kids.

Speaking of breakups, talk about **how you'll handle conflict**. Set expectations for when the inevitable disagreements arise. Talk to your partner about how you handle difficult situations. Do you need space to go off and think about it? Do you prefer to stay engaged in a conversation until you find a resolution? Find a pattern that will work for both of you. This will enable you to handle difficult situations while minimizing blow-ups.

Of course, these conversations about relationship dynamics, future plans, expectations, and goals take a while. But I believe it's useful to consider these issues on your own, outside a relationship, then again if you're considering committing to someone for the long term. If you believe you may have found a keeper, you have every right to start talking about what a future together would look like. It's exciting, talking about building a life together. Enjoy it. If it isn't enjoyable, I'd encourage you to reflect on that.

CAREER PLANNING

Back to your own professional path. Once you've gotten the first job and you are starting to get comfortable in it, you're ready to look at your long-term career goals. Again, while I could write another book just about managing your career, it really boils down to a simple and actionable method.

Create and validate your plan

Creating your plan starts with **setting goals with a time frame**. For example, I wanted to be a CEO. To do that, I needed to get on the fast track. At IBM, that meant becoming a manager of a branch or business unit by the time I was thirty. Your goal doesn't need to look anything like mine, but you need to consider what you want your life to be like in the next decade, in middle age, or beyond. What would you like to accomplish? What are your expectations for your standard of living? Visualize yourself in the future, and write down what you think you want to accomplish and when.

Validating your goals is an important next step. Can you actually achieve the things you've imagined? Is your timeline possible? I'm all for ambitious, aggressive, challenging goals. They just have to be realistic. If I'd decided my goal was to be an astronaut by the time I was thirty, that would not have been realistic. I hadn't studied the sciences; I'd have to go back to school; and I could never do all that and gain the work experience required by thirty. So look for people who have some experience in the areas that interest you, tell them about your goals and timeline, and ask them if your plan sounds reasonable. Then adjust accordingly.

Next, **work backward** to create smaller goals and time frames. For example, knowing that I wanted to be a CEO, I figured I needed to be an executive in my early thirties, heading toward CEO. Therefore, I needed to be a senior manager by thirty. Come up with some intermediate objectives, and again, validate them against real life—can this really happen? Don't forget to factor in other important things, like giving yourself time for family, self-enrichment, and the occasional vacation.

Once you've plotted the milestones you want to cross, it's just a (not-so-simple) matter of **executing your plan**—a process that will take years, if not decades. Be prepared to **adjust as you go**. Remember, life never turns out exactly as you plan. Flexibility and resilience are key, but if you're moving at least somewhat toward your goal, you're doing well.

Build and leverage your network

I've said it before: The very first thing to do once you've set your career goals is to **share those goals**. Share them with your boss, your boss's boss, your colleagues, your advisors…with absolutely everyone. It is risky to talk openly about your ambitions, because it makes you vulnerable—but as I always ask myself, what's the worst that can happen? Can you live with that? Can you live with what happens if you *don't* share your goals? How can people support your success if they don't know what you want?

As soon as you're working, or even before, you can begin to

adopt mentors. Use my method: Don't make formal asks, but rather, just ask simple yes-or-no questions of people you'd like to learn from, then let them know how it goes. When you make it easy for people to give you advice, you make the mentoring dynamic less intimidating for both of you. By applying their advice and following up afterward, you will earn their attention and respect, and when you succeed as a result of their mentorship, they'll be proud of you as well. Don't forget to seek advisors and mentors at your own level and in various areas of your life. Nearly everyone you meet has something they can teach you. And you have something to offer to others, so don't forget to give back.

Developing and nurturing your network is a lifelong process. Integrate it into your lifestyle. The more people you know, the more challenging it will be to keep your connections alive and vibrant; yet the more people you know, the more vibrant and interesting your life can be. For Scotty and me, keeping in touch with our networks is a way of life. I've established a dinner club here in the Bay Area that gets together regularly to share amateur gourmet cuisine—this combines a hobby and networking. A couple of times a year, Scotty and I will go to the ballet or to a show, but instead of just the two of us, we'll invite a big group of friends. I'm talking like fifty people. This turns an outing into an event, it gives us an opportunity to stay in touch with the people we value, and it deepens our connections to our network through shared experiences. Even the people who can't make it to an event know you thought of them, so the invitation alone helps keep relationships alive.

As you plan and execute on your career goals, people are your secret weapon. You are not walking through this world alone, and I can't say this enough: People want to help you succeed. Share your ambitions and your experiences with others, and you will reap the rewards.

HAVING CHILDREN

Eventually, you may want to start a family of your own. If you've followed my advice so far, you've certainly discussed this with your partner, or if you're single, you've considered how you want solo parenthood to work. As the idea of a family gets closer to becoming a reality, here are a few more things to think about.

Before you have children

One of the earliest considerations—after thinking about how many kids you want and when you'll have them—is how to **budget for childcare**. This will look different for every family, but if you're among the majority of parents, you'll need to consider childcare expenses. Decide what kind of childcare you think you'll need, and find out what it will cost. Then create the financial flexibility to be able to afford it by tightening your budget elsewhere. For Scotty and me, childcare was the first chunk we took out of our budget, and we arranged everything else around it—our house, cars, entertainment, and so on. Knowing that our children were well cared for in our absence was our top priority.

I believe that most parents spend a lot of time thinking about what they want for their children in terms of **values**, **education**, and **life experiences**. Far be it from me to tell you how to do this; it is an individual process. I will tell you what worked well for my family: Scotty and I determined before the kids were born that we wanted them to be self-sufficient, confident, and caring. Every parenting decision we made was based on whether it would encourage those values. Likewise, we knew we wanted our kids to have strong educations. We adopted my parents' strategy of moving into the best school districts we could, so our kids would have the best opportunities available. And, of course, we saved toward college funds for both our kids. As for experiences, eventually we wanted them to have a parent at home and engaged with their lives, and we were willing to make the trade-offs to make that happen. We also wanted Kheaton and Kethlyn to get involved in their communities and to build teamwork through sports and activities. I could go on, but you get the picture. You will set your own priorities, and I suggest you set them early—even before the kids arrive in your life. Your priorities will serve as a guiding force for future decisions.

Once you have children

Once you become a parent, life becomes a series of choices and decisions, many of them focused on the short term. By this time, I believe you will know what you want and how to accomplish it, and you will be off on a grand adventure. For the purposes of this book, I'll keep my advice simple.

We've already discussed the importance of **getting help when you need it**. In addition to childcare and, if you have a partner, your partner's support, this could mean asking relatives or friends to chip in or seeking extra help from your church or support groups. Need someone to watch your child while you focus on work one Saturday? Ask a relative or a friend with children to help, and offer to reciprocate. Think ahead whenever possible, and remember to ask for exactly what you need. If you tell people specific ways they can help you, generally they will be glad to do so, especially when you periodically offer something in return. (No one, neither friends nor family, wants to feel used.)

For busy people like you and me, remembering to **be present** is also important. This was easier for Scotty and me; when our children were young, smartphones didn't exist, and the pull to be "always on" was different. Get creative about setting boundaries around family time. Plan ahead for how you will encourage your family to connect on a somewhat regular basis, and in particular, plan for how you will personally hold up your part of the bargain. Being able to be present with your family is a gift and a blessing for all of you.

On the other hand, make sure you are creating **"me" time**. We all need it, and no matter how busy you are, you can find a way to make this work. From the beginning, establish your "me" time as a priority, and if you are partnered, find a way to work in concert with your partner to carve it out. For example, if you love sleeping in just a few extra minutes on the weekends, see if your partner can agree to get breakfast on Saturdays. Your partner may ask you in return to handle dinner or playtime while they get away. If you are a solo parent, seek out others who might watch your children for an evening or overnight, and you can return the favor. Many gyms offer childcare while you exercise or take classes. When your children reach a certain age, you can establish "me" time for both of you—time you each spend alone, even as you're in the same house. The more you incorporate this practice, the healthier it is for everyone.

LONG-TERM LIFE PLANNING

Life really is what happens when you're making other plans. I believe that the way to get the most out of life is to practice **work/life integration**—not *balance*, but a holistic approach that helps you live your life fully every day.

Early in my career, in the 1980s, professional women were encouraged to act like men. I wore suits with silk bow ties, and I did everything I could to hide the fact that I was actually a woman with a family. It was exhausting, particularly because human beings just plain don't work that way. We're not robots who activate certain functions at certain times. We walk through the world as our full selves, all the time.

So how do we practice work/life integration? Each of us comes up with our own formula. For instance, to this day, if I am at work and my kids call, I pick up the phone if I can. If I don't and it's urgent they know I'll pick up if they call right back. Likewise, I have always integrated my married life and work life. In fact, in the early days of MetricStream, when there was no money and I wanted to have a party for the employees, Scotty came down and operated the grill, getting to know everyone in the process. In other areas of my life, I integrate by meeting people to walk and talk, getting a little exercise while we chat. Scotty and I have integrated our hobbies, socializing, and philanthropy, hosting an annual pig roast to benefit the Cypress Mandela Training Center, raising close to $100K per event.

The point is this: Figure out what keeps you feeling happy, whole, and fulfilled, then design your life to integrate the activities that feed you.

Instead of a scale to be balanced, I think of life as a three-legged stool. The three legs are family, work, and community. They work together, and they strengthen each other. If one leg wobbles, the other two keep you upright.

Creating an integrated life plan means just what it sounds like: Your life plan should honor all those parts of yourself. I firmly believe that, if you're willing to do the work, you can have everything you want—but not all at the same time. When I think of my life in phases, I see young mother Shellye did not travel much or go to fancy restaurants, but she had a successful career and a healthy family. Now that my kids have left the nest, I am enjoying traveling with Scotty, having new experiences, and broadening my career. This is how a life plan works: It has room for everything, just not all at once.

You could start designing your life by thinking about **the values you want to live by**. Are you community and service oriented? Family oriented? Creative? An adventurer? Comfort focused? Legacy driven? Identifying key values can guide you toward certain goals. Once you have chosen the experiences or achievements you want to go after, ask yourself, "What are the **key actions** I need to take to accomplish that?" How can you make all the areas of your life work together holistically? It may take some creative problem-solving, but you can do it. Every life is unique, and yours will be an adventure of your own design.

So there it is, my best advice for your best life. Above all else, remember this: Success is not a goal to be reached, but a continuous process. Celebrate your accomplishments, no matter how small. When you reach your goals, set new ones. If you fail to reach a goal, don't beat yourself up; learn your lessons, change your plan, and get going. If you are moving in the direction of your aspirations, every day is a success. Don't ever let yourself forget that.

Epilogue

I finished writing this book at the close of 2018, a year after I ended my tenure at MetricStream. From a little start-up called Zaplet, over fourteen years the company had flourished and exceeded even my expectations. We became a leader in our space. It was time for someone new to take the reins, for me to begin what I now call Phase II of my career.

It won't surprise you that I had planned ahead for this change, back when I was CMO at NorthPoint and approaching forty years old. However, this was different from the planning of my youth—my strict timeline for marriage, motherhood, and career milestones. The plan I made for Phase II included a lot of flexibility. Rather than giving my all to one company, I wanted to take on advisory roles as a board member, consultant, writer, and speaker. This would give me the flexibility and funding to travel the world and enjoy my family—two passions Scotty and I share. I laid the groundwork to launch Phase II as early as age fifty, but I thought I'd keep working through Phase I until I was sixty, maybe sixty-five. Again, even in the timing, my plan was flexible. I left room for the unexpected to happen, and it did.

When Scotty's doctor noticed something unusual in a routine blood test, he encouraged us not to worry too much about it. He explained that MGUS, or monoclonal gammopathy of undetermined significance, usually causes no problems, but a certain percentage of the time it develops into cancer, and not one of the curable ones. He suggested we keep tracking it, but he assured us the risk was small. Scotty was strong as an ox—in great shape, working out at the gym, the picture of health—so we moved forward with confidence.

Three years later, in 2010, Scotty was still his robust, apparently healthy self when he received the diagnosis: incurable blood cancer. Life expectancy: five years from the start of treatment. Could be less. Could be more.

This news set us on our heels, but like we have done with everything, Scotty and I talked it through together. As the one who is always trying to put things in perspective, I said, "You know, we're all dying. We just know now that your time might be sooner than we thought. We're going to do everything we can to fight it and manage it." That's when I told Scotty and our kids, "This is actually a blessing for us. As you know, I believe there's always a blessing, but sometimes you need to look harder for it. Our blessing is that we're going to live a better life. Because we're going to live for the now, and most people don't do that. We're going to do things that we would have waited to do. We're going to do them now." While I thought we were enjoying life as I climbed the ladder, we weren't fully. I had accumulated vacation days, for instance, waiting for the right time to take them. I was putting off trips and experiences for "when the time was right."

The first thing we did? We took a three-week trip to Africa. We could have waited—until we had more time, until the kids had more vacation days. But traveling and visiting with family and friends became our priorities. At the time, I was still carrying the CEO job, and I started taking all my vacation. We decided we're living life first, fighting cancer second.

So, for the next seven years, we focused on living life, while I continued in my capacity at MetricStream. We managed my career and Scotty's treatment with a lot of support from family and friends. In fact, at one point, I thought it might be time to step out of my CEO role. I thought Scotty was dying. He had a bad reaction to chemo. He couldn't eat, couldn't walk. He lost fifty pounds. It was horrible. When he finally stabilized, he was immune compromised, so he wasn't supposed to eat any food that wasn't prepared at home. That's when I told Scotty, "I think I need to step out."

There he was, lying in bed, skin and bones, and he says to me, "If you step out, that means we are living life for cancer, and then what the heck am I fighting for?"

Okay, I thought, *so I can't step out. How am I going to do this?*

When people receive a life-changing health diagnosis, often they don't tell anybody. But how are you going to get the help you need if you don't tell the universe you need it? We made no secret about Scotty's diagnosis. So when we needed help, people showed up. I reached out to friends and to family, and from the end of November until April, we had a family member staying with us. I had a calendar filled with names of people who would fly out and spend whatever time they could with us, taking Scotty back and forth to doctors' appointments. In addition, friends set up a food calendar. People signed up to drop off meals. Now remember, these meals needed to be home cooked, and many of the folks who volunteered were busy people: CEOs and such. They knew they couldn't just order takeout. Yet they all signed up and provided meals, not for a week but for four and a half months. Gratitude doesn't begin to describe how we felt to be on the receiving end of such kindness.

Scotty has had his ups and downs since then, but in spring of 2017 we learned he was in his final stage of cancer. As it turned out, the company was on solid footing after closing a growth capital round. It was time to say goodbye to Phase I and hello to Phase II of my career. Time to find my replacement as CEO and begin writing this book. And because we planned for this, flexibly, we were ready to execute our plan. In Phase II, in addition to my career goals, my new personal goal is to have no regrets.

Not long ago, Scotty and I traveled back home to celebrate my gran's 105th birthday, at a restaurant in Atlanta. One hundred and five, can you believe it? Five generations of my family attended. My parents were there. Mom has a few health challenges now, but she's a fighter and doesn't let anything slow her down. Dad is just as charming as ever, though he doesn't wrestle the young kids anymore. Looking around that banquet room, I couldn't help but think about how far we'd all come—the generations attending the party, and the ancestors who came before us, those whose names appear in our regally embossed family Bible and in the yellowed manumission paper that released my ancestors from slavery.

All of my siblings have earned spots at Ivy League colleges. Lindy is now a professor in the Business School at the University of Florida. Niki is the senior director of human resources for Mars, the candy company. My brother, Arch, whom the world knows as Lester III, is player director of the NFL Players Association.

⌒

Scotty and I are so proud of our children. After making an impact in youth service nonprofits, Kheaton founded Juggernaut Services in New York, where he lives with his fiancée. Kethlyn is currently making her mark at Capgemini while raising my three grandbabies with her husband. We can only imagine where this newest generation will lead us.

Gran had a blast at her birthday party. I called her after, and she kept telling me, "I just can't thank the Lord enough for allowing me to live so long, to see all of my children doing well." To Gran, we're all her children, even the tiny grandbabies. Of course we are.

So much has changed in Gran's lifetime. The struggles she went through to get us to where we are today—some of those struggles, I will never know. She always believed in us, and with that belief and a lot of hard work, she started us all on a journey that led to wonderful accomplishments that may have seemed completely impossible for a black woman in the early twentieth century. Gran and my mother, Mera, didn't let that stop them. They pushed us all to do our best, no matter what.

When I think about the legacy my mother and my grand-mother have created, I start to think about my own. What do I want to leave behind? It's so simple it sounds trite: I want to inspire the upcoming generations and make a positive impact on the world. As long as there are people out there who need encouragement to keep going, to be resilient, and to reach their goals, I want to support them. This is the work I will continue, motivating people to keep pushing against barriers, including the ones in our minds, and to break through to ever better things. I want to see more success and more happiness for women, for minorities, and for everyone else who sets out to find it. I want to give people the tools and the inspiration to reach for the impossible and grab it.

Recently, after speaking about women and leadership at a national conference, I was quickly slipping out of the venue when I heard the sound of high heels, tap, tap, tapping on the tile behind me. I looked back and saw a woman approaching me, almost out of breath. "I just heard you speak, and I had to tell you what an honor it was to hear your perspectives. Your voice is so powerful and most relevant in the world of business. Thank you for your boldness and courage to speak what is real in business for women and people of color. Most people dance around it, and you did not. Your words have impacted my life!"

After thanking this woman for her feedback, I climbed into a Lyft and speed-dialed Scotty to let him know I'd be home early enough to make dinner—something I enjoy doing, and these days I have the time. As I clicked off the call, a deep, satisfied smile slowly emerged. I sank into my seat and gazed contentedly out the window into the beautiful spring afternoon. Right now, everything looks like it is coming alive. The trees appear to be exploding with newly opening buds. Light filters through their branches onto bushes awash in soft pink, white, and orange hues. As the traffic moves and people fade into the scenery, I reflect for a moment on Phase II. This is exactly where I'd hoped I would be. I've traded in an "always-on" CEO position for a portfolio of board seats and advisory roles. I now have flexibility for the first time in over thirty-five years—time to share what I've experienced and learned, time to speak, time to write, time to spend with my husband and family.

My musings are interrupted by a wave of sounds emanating from my iPhone—a FaceTime call from my three grandchildren. "Mimi! Mimi! Where are you?" they shout, their normal greeting.

I answer, "I'm on my way home..."

Book Dedication

The music is playing, competing with the loud hum of excited voices from the wedding guests as they chatter in between bites of dinner. The surroundings are beautiful. We are at the Estate in Buckhead, in Atlanta, Georgia. It is a formal wedding, and everyone is dressed in tuxes, suits, and gowns, backlit by the twinkling candles casting shadows on the walls and arches of the restored nineteenth-century mansion.

My emotions are swirling as I attempt to eat and converse with the family of my nephew's new in-laws. My eldest nephew just said his vows. This is a wonderful, joyous celebration, and yet... I feel waves of sadness off and on. And then it happens. In the background I hear Marvin Gaye's voice crooning "Baby, I'm hot just like an oven... I need some lovin'... And when I get that feeling, I want sexual healing..." My throat tightens, my breathing gets shallow, I feel the tears welling up behind my eyes. I have to escape. I can't lose it right here at the table. I look up and see my son, Kheaton, across the room, looking right at me. He nods sadly, just so slightly. Blinking away tears and trying to breathe more deeply, I jump out of my seat and rush toward the restroom as fast as a long gown and four-inch heels allow me. I feel my daughter, Kethlyn, before I see her. She intercepts, puts her arm around me, and helps me to the restroom, where I fall into her arms sobbing.

It's September 7, just shy of four months since Scotty succumbed to his cancer on May 17. "Sexual Healing" by Marvin Gaye was our song. It was released in 1982, the year we met. I still remember Scotty excitedly calling me in my dorm room.

It was after midnight and I'd been sleeping. Responding to my groggy answer, he urgently said, "Listen!" "What? What's wrong?" I respond, immediately becoming alert and concerned. "Listen to the song!" he insists. *A song, what in the world?* It's a weeknight; I have classes and work tomorrow. "Just listen, this should be our song," he says more tenderly. And so, I listen.

And indeed it became our song. Whenever it played, no matter what we were doing, we'd stop and dance…And now it was playing and he wasn't here…not here to share this milestone of my nephew's wedding, not here to see his daughter act as the officiant for the wedding, won't be here when our engaged son walks down the aisle next year…He's gone, and my grief is still very real.

"It just takes time." That is what everyone who has walked in my shoes tells me. So I have to be patient, patient with myself and patient with the world that goes on. I work hard to stay busy, to create the illusion that time is moving faster.

While Scotty never saw this book in its published form, he read it. In addition to being a book about personal and professional growth, this is also a love story and tribute to my husband. Now the publication and launching of this book is providing me with a much-needed new focus and distraction.

So I dedicate this book to my late husband. After almost thirty-five years of marriage, Scotty will always be a part of me and who I am. In that way...he lives on...

Acknowledgments

I decided over a decade ago that one day I would write this book. I wanted to answer the question I frequently receive: "How did you do it?" Thank goodness I didn't know just how much work and effort it would take when I began.

First and foremost, I want to thank my number one cheerleader, my late husband, Scotty. He read many drafts along the way, reminding me of details and adding his flair to some stories in the way that only he could. He gave me the gift of time, space, and support to be able to write. My daughter, Kethlyn, carved out time to read the book from cover to cover more than anyone else as it evolved. I leaned heavily on Kethlyn and my son, Kheaton, as the book was being finalized and Scotty's health was declining. I am so proud of both of them.

Heartfelt thanks go to my parents, Mera and Lester Archambeau, who answered many random questions and looked up dates and details in support of this book. Their love and support has been unwavering and I'm thrilled they get to see this book published.

I asked a lot of people for help when I started. Thankfully people were generous with their knowledge and time. It began with a conversation with my sister-in-law, Kathleen Archambeau, an author herself, who told me to think of the book as my first book, not "the" book. She cautioned that many inexperienced writers try to squeeze everything into one book and it just doesn't work. This conversation was followed by sessions with other authors who took time to share and give me advice: Caroline Clarke, Meg Waite Clayton, Price Cobb, Nancy Duarte, Ben Horowitz, Alan Eagle, Gay Gaddis, Laura Herring, Guy Kawasaki, Eric Ries, Jonathan Rosenberg, and Chris Yeh.

My writing coach, Jessica Reader, and my editing team at Silicon Valley Press, Joe DiNucci, Atiya Dwyer, and Cheryl Dumesnil, helped me shape my story and lessons learned into a book that I hope you enjoyed.

I want to thank all of my early readers who gave me feedback and great encouragement as the book took shape:

Kene Anoliefo
Kellyn Archambeau
Karsyn Archambeau
Ciara Brown
Price Cobb
Rodney Ellis
Alana Hewitt
Angela Johnson
Amanda Jurist
Jackson Larango
Clare Leinweber
Bernice Malizia
Lowell McAdam
Monica Monroe

Delores Mounsey
Tsedal Neeley
Andrew Overton
Beth Roemer
Heidi Roizen
Sheryl Sandberg
Vikas Sharon
Gunjan Sinha
Riya Sinha
Brad Smith
Beth Stewart
Lisa Stone
Shraddha Varma
Sophia Velastegui
Karl Welsh
Chris Yeh

I also want to thank my literary agent, Jim Levine, and my editor, Gretchen Young, at Hachette Book Group's Grand Central Publishing imprint, both of whom believed in the book and were very supportive.

Finally, I want to thank my village. I never would have had the full life I've lived without the help and encouragement of my extended village over the years: my extended Archambeau and Scott families; the Dallas Bid Whist Group; the East Palo Alto YMCA family; the Gourmet Club; Bill's CEO Group; my C200 sisters; ITSMF; Watermark; my MetricStream, LoudCloud, NorthPoint, Blockbuster, and IBM colleagues; and my friends and neighbors in every place we lived. I am grateful for your love and support.

Notes

2. BEWARE OF IMPOSTOR SYNDROME

1   Lin Bian, Sarah-Jane Leslie, and Andrei Cimpian, "Gender Stereotypes About Intellectual Ability Emerge Early and Influence Children's Interests," *Science* 355, no. 6323 (2017): 389–91, doi:10.1126/science.aah6524.

2   Clark McKown and Rhona S. Weinstein, "The Development and Consequences of Stereotype Consciousness in Middle Childhood," *Child Development* 74, no. 2 (2003): 498–515, doi:10.1111/1467-8624.7402012.

3   Clark McKown and Michael J. Strambler, "Developmental Antecedents and Social and Academic Consequences of Stereotype-Consciousness in Middle Childhood," *Child Development* 80, no. 6 (2009): 1643–59, doi:10.1111/j .1467-8624.2009.01359.x.

9. LEARN THE ROPES

4   Janice M. McCabe, *Connecting in College: How Friendship Networks Matter for Academic and Social Success* (Chicago: University of Chicago Press, 2016).

10. PREPARE FOR OPPORTUNITY TO APPEAR

5   Hostetter, Sabrina Williamson Sullenberger, and Leila Wood, "'All These People Who Can Do Things That I Can't': Adolescents' Reflections on Class, Poverty, and the American Dream," *Journal of Poverty* 19, no. 2 (2015): 133–52, doi:10.1080/10875549.2014.991888.
6   *Survey of the States* (New York: Council for Economic Education, 2016).
7   Tabea Bucher-Koenen, Annamaria Lusardi, Rob Alessie, and Maarten van Rooij, "How Financially Literate Are Women? An Overview and New Insights" (Washington, DC: Global Financial Literacy Excellence Center, 2016).

11. STRATEGIC ON ALL FRONTS

8   Emerging Technology from the ArXiv, "First Evidence That Online Dating Is Changing the Nature of Society," *MIT Technology Review*, October 10, 2017, accessed October 24, 2017,

https://www.technologyreview.com/s/609091/first-evidence
-that-online-dating-is-changing-the-nature-of-society/.

9   "Fact Sheet: The Decline in U.S. Fertility," in *World Population Data Sheet 2012* (Washington, DC: Population
Reference Bureau, 2012), accessed October 24, 2017,
http://www.prb.org/publications/datasheets/2012/world
-population-data-sheet/fact-sheet-us-population.aspx.

12. FOSTER SELF-DETERMINATION

10   Richard M. Ryan and Edward L. Deci, "Self-Determination
Theory and the Facilitation of Intrinsic Motivation, Social De-
velopment, and Well-Being," *American Psychologist* 55, no. 1
(January 2000): 68–78, doi:10.1037//0003-066x.55.1.68.

14. BUILD YOUR REPUTATION

11   Matthew Hutson and Tori Rodriguez, "Dress for Success:
How Clothes Influence Our Performance," *Scientific American*, January 01, 2016, accessed October 24, 2017, https://
www.scientificamerican.com/article/dress-for-success-how
-clothes-influence-our-performance/.

12   Rob Buckley, "Why the Education Sector Is Ripe for Digital
Disruption," I-CIO, January 2015, accessed October 24,
2017, http://www.i-cio.com/management/insight/item/why
-education-sector-is-ripe-for-digital-disruption.

19. DELEGATE

13 U.S. Department of Labor, Bureau of Labor Statistics, Charts by Topic: Household Activities, "American Time Use Survey," Bureau of Labor Statistics, 2015.

14 Leah Ruppanner, "We Can Reduce Gender Inequality in Housework—Here's How," *The Conversation*, May 29, 2016, accessed October 24, 2017, https://theconversation.com /we-can-we-reduce-gender-inequality-in-housework-heres -how-58130.

24. TELL PEOPLE WHAT YOU WANT

15 LeanIn.org and McKinsey & Company, *Women in the Workplace 2016*, McKinsey & Company, 2016.

16 Hannah Riley Bowles, Linda Babcock, and Lei Lai, "Social Incentives for Gender Differences in the Propensity to Initiate Negotiations: Sometimes It Does Hurt to Ask," *Organizational Behavior and Human Decision Processes* 103, no. 1 (2007): 84–103, doi:10.1016/j.obhdp.2006.09.001.

36. BUILD YOUR NETWORK

17 I.J. Hetty van Emmerik, Martin C. Euwema, Myrthe Geschiere, and Marieke F.A.G. Schouten, "Networking

Your Way through the Organization; Gender Differences in the Relationship between Network Participation and Career Satisfaction," *Women in Management Review* 21, no. 1 (2006): 54–66, doi:10.1108/09649420610643411.

39. LIFE PLANNING 101

18 Hannah Devlin, "Maximum Human Lifespan Could Far Exceed 115 Years—New Research," *Guardian*, June 28, 2017, accessed October 24, 2017, https://www.theguardian.com/science/2017/jun/28/maximum-human-lifespan-new-research-mortality.